SABRINA FAIR

THE DRAMA LIBRARY

General Editor: EDWARD THOMPSON

For further details, see end of this book.

SABRINA FAIR

OR

A WOMAN OF THE WORLD

A Romantic Comedy by

SAMUEL TAYLOR

WILLIAM HEINEMANN LTD
MELBOURNE :: LONDON :: TORONTO

FIRST PUBLISHED 1955

PUBLISHED BY
WILLIAM HEINEMANN LTD
99 GREAT RUSSELL STREET, LONDON, W.C.1
PRINTED IN GREAT BRITAIN BY THE PUBLISHERS AT
THE WINDMILL PRESS, KINGSWOOD, SURREY

FOR
SUZANNE
WHO TAUGHT SABRINA TWO THINGS

SCENES

The North Shore of Long Island about an hour from
New York.

ACT I   A Saturday afternoon in September
ACT II   Friday evening, two weeks later

INTERVAL

ACT III   The following morning
ACT IV   Immediately afterwards

CHARACTERS

Maud Larrabee
Julia Ward McKinlock
Linus Larrabee, Jr.
Linus Larrabee
Margaret
David Larrabee
Gretchen
Sabrina Fairchild
Fairchild
A Young Woman
A Young Man
Another Young Woman
Another Young Man
Paul D'Argenson

SABRINA FAIR was first presented in London by Emile Littler and Peter Daubeny at The Palace Theatre, Shaftesbury Avenue, W.1, on 4th August, 1954, with the following cast:

MAUDE LARRABEE	Cathleen Nesbitt
JULIA WARD McKINLOCK	Zena Dare
LINUS LARRABEE, JR.	Ron Randell
LINUS LARRABEE	Allan Jeayes
MARGARET	Gladys Tudor
DAVID LARRABEE	Phil Brown
GRETCHEN	Dorothy Whitney
SABRINA FAIRCHILD	Marjorie Steele
FAIRCHILD	Cyril Luckham
A YOUNG WOMAN	Simone Lovell
A YOUNG MAN	Brian Hankins
ANOTHER YOUNG WOMAN	Vivian Pickles
ANOTHER YOUNG MAN	Antony Carrick
PAUL D'ARGENSON	Paul Hardwick

The play produced by
JOHN CROMWELL

with settings by
DONALD OENSLAGER

PROLOGUE

The music, which is lightly gay and nostalgic and eighteenth century, fades down until it is almost gone.

The stage is in darkness. A pool of light appears slowly, and in it there stands a girl in a simple dress, looking very much as though she were about to go off to a party of sixteen-year-olds.

THE GIRL *speaks*: Once upon a time,
   In a part of America called the North Shore of Long
      Island,
   Not far from New York,
   Lived a very small girl on a very large estate.
   The house on the grounds had many rooms, and many
      servants,
   And in the garage were many cars,
   And out on the water were many boats.
   There were gardeners in the gardens,
   And a chauffeur to drive the cars,
   And a boatman who hauled out the boats in the fall
   And scraped their bottoms in winter
   And put them back in the spring.
   From the windows of her room
   The girl could look out on an indoor tennis court
   And an outdoor tennis court; an indoor swimming pool
   And an outdoor swimming pool
   And a pool in the garden for goldfish.
   Life was pleasant here.
   For this was about as close to heaven as one could get
   On Long Island.
   But then one day the girl grew up
   And went beyond the walls of the grounds
   And found the world.

   The light fades out; THE GIRL *disappears; the music is gone.*

ACT I

The scene is a walled garden. The country house it adjoins forms the left wall of the scene, running on a slight angle off down left. Up left, about two thirds of the way, the house makes a jog out to the right, then runs up upstage. This jog is a small room used as a bar, off the main living room of the house. The main level of the house is above the garden and opens on to a stone terrace about three feet above the ground level. The broad stone steps that lead from the terrace to the garden fit inside the jog, running from the outside wall of the bar downstage some six or eight feet to a graceful iron railing. There is a door from the terrace into the bar facing the audience, and wider, french glass doors in the left wall leading into the main part of the house. The walls are of red brick and indicate a handsome example of a Georgian country house.

This walled garden is rather an open court for living; in Western America it would be called a patio. Upstage, a low red wall topped by grey slate runs from the corner of the house across the stage on a slight angle and off to the right. It is broken just right of centre by a wide opening that gives on the gardens of the property. Beyond the opening, two paths diverge, one leading left into the gardens, the other leading right through the gardens and down the hill to the boathouse. We can see only the beginnings of these paths, for we are on a rise of ground. Beyond the brick wall are shrubs and trees; beyond these, the sky and flashing glimpses of Long Island Sound. The scene goes off right to the tennis court and to the garages.

Since this garden—this courtyard—is a family gathering-place, its furniture is well made and handsome and has an air of permanence.

We are on the edge of Long Island Sound, about an hour from New York City.

It is a Saturday afternoon in September, shortly after lunch; a clear, warm day, with that sparkling brightness peculiar to the seacoast in early autumn.

1

At rise, the scene seems uninhabited, but then we become aware of the figure of a woman in a chaise longue, the upper half shielded from the sun and from us by the canopy which has been pulled well down. To dispel any mystery immediately, let us say that this is JULIA WARD MCKINLOCK, *a woman of fifty-eight who—it will soon be seen—is plain, stocky, squared-off, with straight grey hair that is cut short, and a plain, square face that shows intelligence and good humour and awareness. At the moment, her most prominent feature is her feet.*

After a short time, MAUDE LARRABEE *wanders up from the garden and appears at the opening in the brick wall up centre. She is* JULIA's *age and is, like* JULIA, *a woman of grace and charm and determination. But there the similarity ends.* MAUDE LARRABEE *has been a reigning beauty all her life, and at fifty-eight gives no sign of abdicating. She is fair and blue-eyed, bright and quizzical, and her smile is a devastatingly effective mingling of laughter and rue. She is slender and small-waisted and erect, with a bearing and a walk that makes her seem taller than she is. She has a way of speaking with a wide-eyed candour and directness that makes every remark of hers important beyond its meaning and every new experience of hers new—by definition—under the sun. Those wide eyes and that impressive directness have helped her immeasurably to rule her world.*

Now, as she enters, carrying a basket of freshly-cut chrysanthemums, she instinctively pauses for effect; then, seeing nothing human other than the lower half of JULIA's *body, she crosses to the chaise longue and peers under the canopy.*

MAUDE: Oh! You're awake! Now, Julia, you shouldn't be. (*She straightens up and pushes the canopy up and back.*) My, it gave me a turn to see those eyes peering out at me. You looked like a mole in there.

JULIA: I felt like a mole. I was beginning to burrow back.

MAUDE: How far, Julia? Aren't they beautiful? I've never liked fall flowers—they're so unsettling—but I'm the only one in the country that has these. (*She crosses over to set the basket of flowers on the terrace.*) John-the-gardener's nephew smuggled them out of Japan, and my dear, it was worth

2

to happen would happen. And it did. Sabrina went to Paris to be a file clerk in one of those world-saving American projects called "NATO", or "SHAPE". Wouldn't you know that we Americans would call something that was going to save the world: "SHAPE"? All I can see is a movie star in a low-cut bathing suit, leaning forward.

JULIA: A democratic gesture.

LINUS LARRABEE, JR. *appears at the centre opening in the back wall. He is in his late thirties, well-set-up, rugged-looking, and easy in his movements.*

LINUS: How are you feeling, Aunt Julia?

JULIA: Tip top.

He wanders across the top of the terrace towards the bar. LINUS is not at all handsome in the conventional terms, but his features are bold and challenging, and he gives an attractive sense of calm and quiet and reserve. He seems always to be holding himself in, checking his laughter and relishing it alone. He is aware of his power and capabilities; it would take a great deal to shake him. He is dressed in white sneakers, an old pair of grey flannels, and an extremely old and well-worn navy-blue yachting jacket. The shirt is white, but there is no necktie. He wears a battered old blue yachting cap.

MAUDE: Oh. Linus. I thought you were out on the Sound.

LINUS: I've been putting the sails on.

JULIA: How's business, Linus?

LINUS: Business is good. How's business with you?

JULIA: Couldn't be better. I read an article about you in *Fortune*, the other day. It said you have organizational know-how.

LINUS: I didn't know it showed. I'll have to speak to my tailor.

He goes into the bar.

MAUDE (*as she crosses with the glass of water*): Really, this mutual admiration society. Julia, did you know that he flew back from South America the minute he heard you'd gone to the hospital?

JULIA: You don't know the half of it. Every time I rolled

5   B

over, he had four more doctors standing there. I must have the most expensive incision in history. I think it was the doctor from Boston who hit the jackpot.

MAUDE: I don't think Linus would have dropped his business for anyone but you, Julia.

JULIA: Or you. Or his father. Or his brother. Don't sell your elder son short, Maude. He may not be much a part of the family, but he'll always be around when you want him.

MAUDE: Yes, I know. But isn't it strange, Julia. David is so completely my child; Linus never belonged to me. Linus never belonged to anyone. I've always had the feeling he's a throw-back to some free and independent Larrabee who sailed out of Newburyport in the slave trade and was probably a bit of a freebooter on the side.

JULIA: Have you seen much of him lately?

MAUDE: Oh, he comes out weekends to sail, when he's in this part of the country. And he is good about family dinners.

From the house, a peremptory man's voice calls: "Maude! Maude!", and then LINUS LARRABEE, SR., *appears on the terrace. He is in his late sixties, a spare, slender man of considerable presence and charm. Since he lost interest in most features of his life many years ago, he is inclined to vagueness about occurrences in the present that do not directly concern him, and has become increasingly taciturn, being given to abrupt silences that he shatters abruptly. He carries himself well. He is essentially a courtly and a gracious man.*

LARRABEE: Maude! Where the devil's Fairchild?

MAUDE: He's gone to meet a train, dear.

LARRABEE: He knows he's to drive me to a funeral.

MAUDE: Yes, dear. He'll be back shortly.

LARRABEE: I don't like waiting about.

MAUDE: Now, Linus, you're only going to Oyster Bay. And the funeral isn't until four o'clock.

LARRABEE: I want to get a good seat.

JULIA: How many funerals this week, Linus?

6

LARRABEE: Two. It's been a damned thin week.

JULIA: Too bad you can't get in a double-header today.

 LINUS *comes out of the bar*.

LARRABEE: Oh, Linus, Rodney Williams is putting up the *Frolic* for sale. I said you might be interested.

LINUS: Now, father, what would I want with a hundred and six foot yawl?

LARRABEE: What's wrong with owning a hundred and six foot yawl?

JULIA: That's a good question.

LARRABEE: It is a very good question, Julia. Why should this world we live in make us ashamed to own the things we can afford?

JULIA: I stand on the Fifth Amendment.

LARRABEE (*to* LINUS): I told Rodney we'd come over tomorrow and go out with him for the day.

LINUS: I have business appointments tomorrow, father.

LARRABEE: Tomorrows' Sunday.

LINUS (*smiling*): I sometimes work on Sunday. But I'll tell you what I'll do with you. I'll go out with you tomorrow morning in the sailing dinghys, and race you around the cove, so you can prove you've still the best sailor on Long Island Sound.

MAUDE (*brightly*): Yes, Linus! You'll enjoy that!

LARRABEE: This is serious. The *Frolic* is the nicest yawl on the Eastern coast. I don't like to see all the big boats being sold out of the Sound. You should have a sense of responsibility about these things.

LINUS: I'm sorry, father.

LARRABEE: What is it you have to do tomorrow that's so important?

LINUS: Just . . . business.

LARRABEE: Is it the plastics thing?

LINUS (*suddenly sharply alert*): Where did you hear that?

LARRABEE: There's a rumour around that you're going into plastics.

LINUS (*sharply*): Who'd you hear it from?

7

LARRABEE: Fisher Boyd. He asked me if it was true.

LINUS: What did you say?

LARRABEE: That I didn't know.

LINUS: That's fine.

He wanders away.

LARRABEE: I would like to know, from time to time, what goes on in the company that bears my name. Is it true?

LINUS: I'd rather you were able to go on saying you didn't know.

LARRABEE crosses to him.

LARRABEE: Is that all the answer you'll give me?

LINUS: Yes. (*Pause.*)

LARRABEE (*calmly*): I am sorry to find your mistrust of the world extends to your father. I will accept the rebuff, since I can do nothing about it. I will say to you that in my world you are admired for the things you do, but not for the way you do them.

He turns and walks into the house.

MAUDE: Linus.

LINUS (*angry with himself*): I'm sorry, I am sorry. I'll make my peace.

He runs into the house after his father. The TWO WOMEN *look at each other.*

JULIA: Nothing serious.

MAUDE: No, they even do that over a game of chess. But I wish they wouldn't. Actually, he's proud of his son. But he hates the word "ruthless". And it's so often applied. (*She looks over at the garage impatiently*.) I do wish Fairchild would come back.

JULIA: Do I remember her?

MAUDE: Who?

JULIA: The girl. Fairchild's daughter.

MAUDE: Sabrina? I don't know. Do you? You should. She's lived here all her life, over the garage. Fairchild's been our chauffeur for thirty years. Of course you know her, Julia. That dun-coloured, sallow little wisp that used to cut around corners when she saw you coming? Very timid, very shy, quite intelligent, and as I recall, terribly athletic. At least, she used to spend most of her time climbing trees. What do you suppose that's a sign of?

JULIA: A vitamin deficiency of some sort. Why is she coming home?

MAUDE: I don't know. Fairchild didn't say. I suppose she got fed up with Paris after five years. She couldn't have had much fun.

JULIA: You didn't give her any letters when she went.

MAUDE: Now, Julia, how could I? Would you write to Madge de Lessac and say, "Dear Countess, this is to introduce my chauffeur's daughter, please give her a whirl?"

LINUS *appears from the house at ease again.*

LINUS: All's well. I've promised to look at that hundred and six foot yawl. (*He smiles wryly.*) With a crew of ten. Am I forgiven?

MAUDE: Yes. But you do devil your family, so.

LINUS (*with a grin*): You tempt me, so, mother.

He kisses her on the top of the head. She pats his hand. Then she sees MARGARET, *the maid, busy at something within the house.*

MAUDE: Oh, Margaret! Take those flowers, will you? And ask Jessie to fix them and put them in the library. (MARGARET *has come out on the terrace, and picks up the basket of flowers.*) Aren't they lovely, Margaret? Tell Jessie she must think of something magnificent to do with them.

MARGARET: Yes, madam.

MAUDE: On second thought, Margaret! Tell her to put them in the living room under me. Under the portrait. And Margaret, while I was in the garden I thought I heard the phone ring.

MARGARET: It was for Mr. Linus, Madam. (*And then, though the information has not been sought.*) It was Mrs. David Larrabee.

LINUS (*coldly*): You gave me the message, Margaret.

MARGARET: I'm sorry, sir.

And with great dignity, she walks into the house. LINUS

9

looks across his mother to JULIA *with a wry smile.*

LINUS: Here we go again.

MAUDE: Does David know that you've been going about with Gretchen quite a bit, lately?

JULIA: Linus, what do I owe you for that operation?

MAUDE (*coldly*): Don't change the subject.

(*She takes the glass of water from* JULIA *and crosses to replace it on the table.*

LINUS: A life-time subscription to your magazine. I always forget to buy it on the news-stand.

MAUDE: Well, Linus? Does David know that you've been going about with Gretchen quite a bit, lately?

LINUS: It's common knowledge, isn't it?

MAUDE: I know. And the servants know. And people who read Cholly Knickerbocker and Mr. Winchell's column, know. I just wondered if David knows.

LINUS: I'll be glad to tell him.

MAUDE: After all, he was married to Gretchen.

LINUS: He's not any more. What is it that troubles you, mother? A man takes out his brother's ex-wife; it certainly isn't incestuous.

MAUDE: It's certainly in questionable taste.

LINUS: Ah, then it's not a matter of morals, it's a matter of etiquette. We don't consult the family priest, we turn to the family bible, Emily Post.

JULIA: Amen.

MAUDE: I hate the new fashion of making fun of the amenities.

LINUS: I'm just trying to get at a basic truth, mother. Am I wrong in going about with Gretchen, or merely wrong in letting it get into the papers? What would you say, Aunt Julia?

JULIA: In matters of this sort, I always ask myself: "What would Lord Byron say?" It puts everything in the proper perspective.

DAVID LARRABEE *wanders out on to the terrace holding a stop watch on a lanyard.*

DAVID: Hey, Linus, I've got your stop watch.

> DAVID *is like* LINUS *in many ways, but is gayer, and at the same time lacks the power, the resolution, and the confidence. He is slim, fair, and has inherited his mother's grace and looks. He has the easy good humour that marks* LINUS, *and the same way of moving easily, with sure control.*

LINUS: I'm not racing today, David; just sailing.

DAVID: On the *International?*

LINUS: No, I put the sails on the *Vimsa.*

DAVID: I might come along. How are you feeling, Aunt Julia?

JULIA: Bully.

> DAVID *smiles at his mother.*

DAVID: I like those flowers, mother.

MAUDE: Aren't they lovely?

DAVID: They set you off beautifully. Or rather, you set them off beautifully.

MAUDE: Thank you, David.

DAVID (*to* LINUS): How soon are you going?

LINUS: As soon as my guest arrives. I don't think it would be any fun for you, David.

DAVID: Oh, have you got a girl coming? (LINUS *nods.*) Then you don't want me along. Does she know enough about a boat to handle the ketch with you alone?

LINUS: Yes, she's pretty good.

DAVID: Then you certainly don't want me along. (*With a knowing grin.*) There's hardly any wind. You may never get home.

LINUS: It's a chance I'll have to take.

DAVID: It's a chance you've taken before.

MAUDE (*carefully*): Linus, who is this girl you're taking sailing? Anyone we know?

DAVID: Yes, who is it?

JULIA (*cutting in*): You know,—I've been wondering for some time how old you boys have to be before you stop calling me Aunt Julia.

DAVID: What should we call you? Miss McKinlock?

JULIA: Well, my only relationship to you is the fact that I roomed with your mother at college; I think you're old enough now to call me by my first name.

DAVID: Too familiar.

JULIA: I'll settle for "Hey, you".

LINUS: Too formal.

DAVID: No, you're stuck with Aunt Julia, Aunt Julia.

MARGARET *appears on the terrace.*

MARGARET: Mrs. David Larrabee.

DAVID (*startled*): What?

GRETCHEN LARRABEE *appears on the terrace. She is* DAVID'S *age. She is strikingly, carefully, immaculately beautiful, with the calm air and the hard sheen of a fashion drawing. She is well-bred, she is knowing, she is tough. And she is a juicy morsel. She wears well-cut shorts, a well-unbuttoned shirt, and carries a pouch and a cardigan sweater.*

GRETCHEN: Hello. It's so long since I've been here, I thought I should have myself announced. Hello, David, how have you been?

DAVID (*puzzled*): Is there something you wanted to see me about?

GRETCHEN: No. (*She descends the steps and goes to* MAUDE, *addressing* LINUS *as she goes.*) I'm sorry I'm late; did you get my message? (*He nods.*) Hello, Mother Larrabee. It's wonderful to see you again.

MAUDE: Hello, Gretchen! How nice you look! (*They kiss politely.*) Did you drive out from town?

GRETCHEN: No, I'm staying with the Hawkin's, in Syosset. You remember Lisa Hawkins.

MAUDE: Yes, of course! Do you know Miss McKinlock?

GRETCHEN: Yes, of course! (*She crosses and shakes hands with* JULIA.) Hello, Miss McKinlock, how've you been?

JULIA: Not well, I've had an operation.

GRETCHEN (*startled*): Oh! Oh, I'm sorry! (*She glances at* LINUS, *who is enjoying the situation quietly.*) You want to go, don't you? (*To* MAUDE.) Will I see you when we get back? I'd love to sit and talk for a while.

MAUDE (*politely*): Yes, dear, perhaps we can have a cup of tea. Ask someone to find me.

GRETCHEN: It's so nice to be going out on the *Vimsa* again. And it's just the way I like it: almost no breeze at all.

She smiles at them all and goes out through the garden.

LINUS (*impassively*): Well. . . .

He nods to his mother without expression, then follows GRETCHEN *into the garden and down the path.*

DAVID: What the hell's this all about?

MAUDE (*embarrassed*): They're going sailing.

DAVID: Why?

MAUDE: They . . . like sailing.

DAVID: Now, come on, mother, what's going on?

MAUDE: Nothing's going on, David—I don't think. Linus has been seeing quite a bit of Gretchen lately, and——

DAVID: How do you know?

MAUDE: It's common knowledge.

DAVID: Why didn't I know?

MAUDE: You read the *New York Times*.

He lets the news sink in, then shakes his head, ruefully.

DAVID: Ah, hell! Do you mean he's in the columns? With my wife? I suppose everyone knows they're having an affair except me.

MAUDE: You've no reason to call it an affair, dear.

DAVID: What would you call it?

MAUDE: Well, anyway, she's not your wife.

At which DAVID *has to laugh.*

DAVID: He brought her here deliberately just to get a rise out of us, didn't he?

MAUDE: Not out of you; out of me. (*Smugly.*) But he didn't get it. My, he does have a barbaric sense of humour.

DAVID: Do you think he'll ever settle down to be a sober citizen?

JULIA: He is a sober citizen; he makes a lot of money.

DAVID: Is that your definition, Aunt Julia?

JULIA: Not mine; the world's. He doesn't have to be what you call a sober citizen because he is an unusually productive citizen. He took a settled old American family business and built it into an international empire before he was thirty-five. When a man is enterprising and successful in the things that matter, like money, the world allows him his small eccentricities in the things that don't matter, like women.

DAVID (*his good humour restored*): You'd better explain that to Gretchen, because she's going to get taken for a ride.

He offers a cigarette to JULIA.

JULIA: Forbidden.

MAUDE: Are you sure, David? Gretchen's a clever girl. And she'd give her eye teeth to nail Linus down. She didn't mind divorcing you, so much, since we made it worth her while, but she hated like the devil divorcing our boats.

JULIA: Charming girl.

MAUDE (*agreeing*): Isn't it sad? So young and pretty. And so very well brought up. And such a very cold fish.

DAVID (*easily*): But not as smart as you think. She wants to be a big operator, and she works at it, but she's an amateur compared to Linus. No girl's ever going to nail him down. You can be sure Linus has been two jumps ahead of her all the way along—and laughing. He hasn't made a false move since he was three.

A pause as he smiles, thinking of LINUS.

JULIA (*abruptly*): David, do you dislike your brother?

MAUDE: Why, Julia! What an idea!

DAVID (*smiling*): I remember reading about that in college, Aunt Julia. What is it they call it among you intellectuals? Sibling rivalry?

JULIA: That's right. It's all the rage among us intellectuals.

LARRABEE *comes out of the house, looking at his watch.*

DAVID: I like him more than any man I've ever known. I always have.

LARRABEE: Who's this you're so fond of?

DAVID: My brother.

LARRABEE: That's a praiseworthy sentiment, David. But

it's not the sort of thing one says out loud. Where is Linus? I want to talk to him about the yawl.

MAUDE: He's gone sailing with Gretchen.

LARRABEE: Gretchen? David's Gretchen?

MAUDE: Well——

LARRABEE (*affably*): I haven't seen Gretchen in some time, David. Where have you been keeping her?

MAUDE: Linus, David and Gretchen are divorced.

LARRABEE: Oh. Oh, yes. (*To* DAVID.) Why did you do that?

DAVID: We discovered we didn't like each other.

LARRABEE: I should think you could have discovered that without getting married. What's she doing here?

DAVID: She's gone sailing with Linus.

LARRABEE: Well, you can't object to that; he's the best sailor on Long Island Sound. (*To* MAUDE.) Why did he go to the station?

MAUDE (*startled*): Who?

LARRABEE: Fairchild.

MAUDE: To meet his daughter. You remember, dear. Sabrina was arriving this morning, on the *Ile de France*.

LARRABEE: Sabrina. Is Fairchild's daughter named Sabrina? I thought it was Della.

MAUDE: No, Della was her mother, our cook.

LARRABEE: Oh, yes. I miss Della.

MAUDE: So do we all.

LARRABEE: But it was a good funeral. We gave it just the right tone; simple, unpretentious, but dignified.

JULIA: No cook could ask for more.

MAUDE (*quickly*): Linus, don't you think you could drive yourself to the funeral this afternoon? It seems a shame to drag Fairchild off as soon as he gets home, when he hasn't seen his daughter in five years.

LARRABEE: Five years. Why would anyone want to live in Europe for five years?

JULIA: I'll be glad to answer that question.

MAUDE: It's no effort to drive to Oyster Bay, Linus. Why

don't you take David's little English car? You enjoy driving it so.

LARRABEE (*with cold precision*): Maude: Lyman Ward, who was my friend and who now lies dead in Oyster Bay, once observed that man's progression through this world is a series of indignities. He is born in an undignified manner, is married as an insignificant part of a female ritual, procreates in a grotesquely undignified position, and spends the rest of his life being ignored by his issue. In the light of this it was Lyman's belief—and it is mine—that it is a man's duty and the duty of his friends to see to it that his exit from this world, at least, shall be made with all possible dignity. It is very little, but it is all that is left. I do not, therefore, propose to drive up to the church in Oyster Bay dressed in white flannels and a school blazer, perched up in an English two-seater. (*He starts for the bar.*) How do you feel, Julia?

JULIA: Ripping.

He goes into the bar. MAUDE *looks after him with amused affection, then smiles at* DAVID.

MAUDE: I hope you can do that when you're seventy. My, when I think of him as he was in the early years. . . . (*She smiles, thinking back.*) There was a time when people knew how to talk, and dinner parties were exciting. . . .

JULIA: He's not seventy, is he?

MAUDE: He will be, in January. Julia, I think you should let up on Linus a bit.

JULIA: In what way?

MAUDE: You catch him up on all the little things he says that he doesn't really mean; you always have.

JULIA: It's because he means them. Your husband is one of the wittiest men I've ever known. He is also one of the stuffiest.

MAUDE (*denying it*): Oh!

DAVID: Can the two go together?

JULIA: They can and they do. It is possible to find the world funny and not one's self. If anyone else went trotting off to every funeral he could find, like a morbid bird dog, your father would have something quite sharp to say about him, I'm sure.

MAUDE: Morbid! He's not a bit morbid, Julia! When he gave up sailing, and sold the schooner, his doctor told him he ought to take up another hobby, so he took up going to funerals. There's nothing morbid about that.

JULIA: No, no. Sort of gay.

MAUDE: It gets him out among people. And it keeps him out in the open air; he always goes along to the cemetary.

JULIA (*to* DAVID): Your mother is the only person I know who can make a preoccupation with death sound like good, clean fun.

MAUDE: Oh, what nonsense! Preoccupation with death, indeed! Come take your nap. I can always tell when you're tired; you begin to sound like the voice of doom. David? (*She starts hauling* JULIA *out of the chaise longue and* DAVID *hurries to help.*) I'll never forget the fashion article she wrote that began: (*She quotes with foreboding.*) "Women's fashions, this fall, will reflect the tensions of the times." I went right out and bought six frivolous hats. David, get the medicine.

DAVID *crosses to get the medicine.*

JULIA (*with good humour, as she and* MAUDE *start for the house*): Thank you, Maude, I prefer to walk alone.

MAUDE *ignores this, and puts her arm through* JULIA'S *as though it were the most natural thing in the world. They get part way across when they are arrested by a call from off right. A young feminine* VOICE, *bright and excited, calls* "Hello!" *eagerly. They stop and turn and look off to the right, and once again the call comes, almost anxiously this time:* "Hello!"

MAUDE (*puzzled*): Who's that?

And as if in answer, the owner of the voice runs on to the scene. SABRINA FAIRCHILD *is about* DAVID'S *age, and will look very much as she does now when she is very much older; for she is one of the lucky ones in whom youth and age will never be measured by days and years. She is beautifully and taste-*

fully and expensively dressed in travelling clothes that show off a very good figure. No one could look more chic. She is not pretty, but her face is appealing and bright with animation and reflects the inner glow of a girl in love; for SABRINA FAIRCHILD *has fallen in love with the world and is carrying on a passionate affair with it. Now, as we first see her, her face is a galaxy of complicated emotions. She is eagerly happy to see these people whom she adores, but she is shy, too, for they are not her family, and the past five years have not altogether dissipated the shyness that was ingrained from childhood. This trace of shyness, however, is not apparent to the people who watch her come towards them. She goes directly to* MAUDE.

SABRINA: Oh, hello! Oh, I'm so glad to see you!

And she stops dead in front of MAUDE *with a great smile of anticipation, and waits to be greeted in return.*

MAUDE (*tentatively, after a moment*): Sabrina . . .?

SABRINA (*brightly*): Yes, of course!

MAUDE (*just as brightly*): Yes, of course! It's Sabrina! Why, Sabrina, I didn't recognise you! Welcome home, my dear!

She puts out her hands, and SABRINA *takes them enthusiastically.*

SABRINA: Oh, I was hoping you wouldn't recognise me! Have I changed? Have I really changed? (*She backs up a bit, hanging on to* MAUDE's *hands.*) I'm so glad to see you! David, you didn't recognise me, either, did you? (*He shakes his head, fascinated.*) Ah! Then I have changed, haven't I? I don't mean just the clothes, that's easy. But me! Myself! Do I seem very different? Here! Now! Without the hat! (*And she tears off the smart, ridiculous little hat, and shakes out her hair.*) Now!

MAUDE (*a bit shell-shocked*): Now more than ever.

SABRINA: How wonderful! I wanted so to hear you say that. Is that vain of me? I don't mean it to sound vain. I just thought it would be such fun to hear you say it. Because I *feel* so different! It was the first thing I thought of when I woke up this morning, as the ship was coming up the bay. And then later, lying in my berth, having breakfast—

18

—my last breakfast of that good French bread and that horrible coffee that I love so—I thought: (*She closes her eyes and tells her dream, with a soft smile.*) What fun it will be . . . they'll all be in the garden, in the walled garden off the terrace . . . and I'll come running in to them to say hello. And they'll say: "Sabrina? Is it Sabrina? Why, Sabrina, we didn't recognise you!" (*She opens her eyes and grins.*) And that's the way it happened! Ah! I think if you had just said, "Oh, hello, Sabrina, how are you?", I'd have died. (*She whirls on* JULIA.) You don't remember me, but I remember you. I used to peek around corners at you.

JULIA: I remember you very well. You used to climb trees, too.

SABRINA: Yes, I did. You're famous in Paris, did you know that? I kept hearing about you all the time. It seems as though everybody knows you. And they tell such wonderful stories about you, in the twenties: about you and Picasso and Gertrude Stein, and the book shop you ran, and the magazine . . . It must be fun to be part of a legend.

JULIA: I think the legend has been exaggerated a bit over the years.

SABRINA: Oh, no! Paris was the most exciting place in the world, then, wasn't it?

JULIA (*smiling*): Yes, it was.

    She likes this girl very much.

SABRINA: It still is. (*She turns and yells.*) Father? (*Her* FATHER *appears at the side, dressed in chauffeur's livery, carrying his cap.* TOM FAIRCHILD *is a stocky, grey-haired man of fifty-five, and at this moment he looks uneasy. A slim book of the Modern Library—Everyman's Library sort sticks up out of his coat pocket.*) I wish you could have seen father at the station. He was completely baffled. There I was, charging across the platform at him, yelling, "Father!", and he kept looking over his shoulder to see who my father was! (*She crosses to him swiftly, smiling at him lovingly.*) I finally

had to leap at him to make him recognise me, didn't I?
And the most terrible thing happened! I leaped too hard
and knocked him down! Right there in front of all Glen
Cove! Father! The most dignified man on Long Island!
(*She gives him an affectionate peck on the cheek.*) Thank good-
ness it wasn't a commuters' train.

FAIRCHILD (*coldly*): Put on your hat, Sabrina.

SABRINA: Oh! (*She looks over to the others anxiously.*) Am I
being too . . . too. . . .

MAUDE: No, dear, of course not.

SABRINA: It's just that I'm so excited. (*With rueful humour,
softly, to her father.*) I'm sorry, father. I shall keep my
place as soon as I know it. But for now, do be an angel
and get that thing out of the station wagon for me. You
know: —— the —— (*She secretly mouths the word* "bird"
at him, and urges him off.)——I want to give it to her now.
And be careful of it, please! (*She watches him go, with a fond
smile, then turns back to* MAUDE.)——I brought you something from Paris. Do you mind? It was given me by a
beau, and I fell madly in love with it. And then I knew I
would have to bring it home to you.

MAUDE: You shouldn't have, Sabrina.

SABRINA: I know. But I wanted to.

MAUDE: I should think your beau would mind.

SABRINA: No. I told him. He didn't mind after I told him
about you. (*With deep affection.*) It's something I hope
will make you laugh. I wanted to bring it to you because
I remembered how you laughed and how I loved so to
hear you when I was a little girl.

MAUDE: Oh.

SABRINA (*softly*): Isn't it strange of the English language,
and typical, that there is no feminine analogue of "hero
worship?"

MAUDE (*moved*): That's very sweet, Sabrina.

    LARRABEE *appears on the terrace.*

LARRABEE: Fairchild? Maude, what the devil's become of
him?

MAUDE: He'll be with you in a moment, Linus. He's just returned.

LARRABEE: I'd planned to be started by now.

SABRINA: Hello, Mr. Larrabee!

LARRABEE: Good afternoon, Gretchen. I'm delighted to see you again.

MAUDE: Now, Linus, does she look like Gretchen?

LARRABEE: Since I haven't the faintest recollection of what Gretchen looked like, I couldn't say. Who are you, young lady?

SABRINA: Sabrina Fairchild!

LARRABEE: Sabrina? Really? (*He looks at* MAUDE; *She nods*.) Ah, you must forgive an old man, Sabrina. I have reached that sad period of old age when all pretty young women look alike.

SABRINA: How very sad for the young women, sir.

LABARREE (*impressed*): Will you come a little closer, please? (SABRINA *darts across and stops before the steps*.) I would *like* to remember you the next time I see you. (*He glances at* MAUDE.) No one like this ever lived over our garage. (SABRINA *laughs*.) But if you say you are Sabrina, I must believe you. And I am happy to see you back, Sabrina. Now, will you tell your father I am waiting for him, my dear? And ask him to bring the big car round.

    He nods and goes into the house, leaving SABRINA *with the laugh hanging. She watches him go with some amazement, then turns back to the others with raised eyebrows and a quizzical smile.*

SABRINA: He sold his schooner, didn't he? Why did he sell it?

MAUDE: He decided there was no one left to sail with.

SABRINA: Oh?

DAVID (*easily*): Father has always explained to us that you can do business with anyone, but you can only sail a boat with a gentleman.

SABRINA (*blithely*): How lonely you must be! Ah, there it is! (*She skips across the stage, calling*.) I'll take it, father! Mr.

Larrabee wants you! You're to bring the big car around right away! (*By now she is offstage, but we can still hear her.*) And please don't worry about me. I'll be all unpacked and respectable when you get back.

> MAUDE *and* DAVID *are watching her.*

MAUDE: What is that she has?

DAVID: It looks like a cage.

JULIA: Don't tell me she's brought you her beau.

> SABRINA *runs on, and it is a cage she carries: a great, magnificently rococo white wire birds cage out of the nineteenth century. Within the cage, calm, proud, sedate, sits a brilliantly coloured cockatoo.*

SABRINA: Here he is! Isn't he beautiful? His name is Maurice.

MAUDE: *Sabrina*, how beautiful!

DAVID: I never saw a parrot like that.

SABRINA: No, a cockatoo. And the most beautiful cockatoo in the world, aren't you, *mon chouchou*? Do you like him? Ah, but I haven't told you! He doesn't talk; not a word. He sings! Yes! He has a beautiful whisky tenor. Oh, I do hope you like him!

MAUDE: But what a magnificent gift! Sabrina! I should think it would break your heart to give him up!

SABRINA: Ah, no, I want you to have him. Please. He'll be such fun for you. He's terribly bright, and he loves to sing. Maurice, this is your new mistress. Will you sing for the lady?

JULIA: What does he sing?

SABRINA: Nursery songs! He has a marvellous repertoire of French nursery songs. I don't know where he learned them. But you haven't lived until you've been wakened in the morning by a cockatoo, singing: (*She sings*) "*Il etait un' bergere, Et ron ron ron, Petit patapon——*" Come on, Maurice! "*Il etait un' bergere, Qui gardait ses moutons, ron ron, Qui gardait ses moutons.*"

> *She waits expectantly.*

THE BIRD: Aaaarrk.

DAVID: He needs tuning.

SABRINA: He's shy, that's the trouble.

JULIA: He's French, that's the trouble. Do you usually speak English to him?

SABRINA: No, of course not! That's it! Really, how stupid. (*She turns back to the bird, and in fluent, darting French addresses him.*) *Ah, mon p'tit, ca te gene devant les Americains, n'est-ce pas? Comme je suis bete! Mais, ne t'inquiete—pas, mon tresor.* (MAUDE *looks at* JULIA *with raised eyebrows, impressed by the girl's fluency.*) *Cette belle dame qui sera ta maitresse est adorable! Regards-la! Une vraie duchesse! Et riche! Oh! C'est fantastique! Tu auras une vie formidable! Et maintenant, tu chanteras un peu, n'est-ce pas?* (*By now, the three spectators are caught up by the intensity of Sabrina's pleading, and are pulling for the bird to join her in song.* SABRINA *sings, beating out the time with a clenched fist.*) *"Sur le pont d'Avignon, l'on ye danse, l'on ye danse, Sur le pont d'Avignon, L'on ye danse tout en ronde."* (*She waits, Silence from the bird.*) Maurice! (*He grooms himself.*) O, dear, I could cry! Honestly! He sings like a bird!

DAVID: I wondered about that.

MAUDE: Do you suppose I intimidate him?

SABRINA: How could you?

JULIA: Of course you intimidate him! He doesn't know anything about you. Except that you're rich. Speak to the bird!

MAUDE: *Bonjour*, Maurice.

SABRINA (*hopefully*): He might sing if *you* started a song for him, just to make him feel at home.

MAUDE (*retreating*): Oh, I hardly think——

DAVID (*amused*): Yes, that's obviously what he's waiting for, mother.

JULIA: Go ahead, Maude.

MAUDE: Well . . . does he know this one? (*She sings.*) *"Au clair de la lune——"*

SABRINA: Of course!

MAUDE:——*"Mon ami Pierrot, Prete-moi ta plume, pour ecrire——"* (*No co-operation from the bird. She gives up.*)

JULIA: Here, let me try. (*She approaches the cage and addresses the bird firmly.) Ecoute, mon vieux! Pas de blagues! Je te connais bien, toi! Je veux que tu chantes avec moi, tu comprends? Eh bien! Allons-y! (She sings.) "Auprès de ma blonde——"*

MAUDE: Julia! That is not a nursery song!

JULIA: It always seemed to me as though it should be. Besides, I suspect this bird of hidden talents. *Alors, mon vieux! "Auprès de ma blonde, Qu'il fait bon fait bon fait bon, Auprès de ma blonde——"*

> *She stops as she sees* SABRINA *staring past her to the terrace.* MARGARET, *the maid, stands there holding a sweater.*

SABRINA (*lovingly*): Ah, Margaret!

MARGARET (*not quite sure*): Sabrina?

> SABRINA *dashes across and up the steps, and throws herself into the woman's arms.*

SABRINA: Ah, Margaret, I'm so glad to see you!

> MARGARET *drops the sweater.*

MARGARET (*holding her close, letting the tears flow without reserve*): Sabrina. . . .

SABRINA (*mistily*): Yes, Margaret, I'm home . . . I've come home. . . .

MARGARET: You were so far away!

SABRINA: I know. But I'm home, now. Don't cry, Margaret. It isn't anything to cry about, is it?

MARGARET: You've come home such a beautiful lady!

SABRINA: Please don't cry, Margaret.

MARGARET: No, no, I'll be stopping, now. (*She makes an effort to pull herself together, and looks over at* MAUDE.) I beg your pardon, Madame. (*But another look at* SABRINA *brings on new freshets.*) My little Brina . . .!

> SABRINA *puts an arm about her and leads her into the house.*

SABRINA (*as they go*): Come along, now. I want to see Jessie and the others. You look wonderful, Margaret. You *have* lost weight! I've brought you a lovely handbag to go with your black satin. And oh, Margaret, a hat! A real Paris hat for you to wear to church on Sundays! Wait 'til you see it! It's the most beautiful hat!!

She laughs at the memory of the hat, and without a backward glance at the others, completely intent on MARGARET, *she leads the woman into the house. The three look after them, saying nothing. Finally:*

MAUDE (*moved*): She does look like a lady.

JULIA: She may even be a lady.

MAUDE (*flaring*): Oh, Julia, don't be such a woman of the people! You know very well what I meant.

JULIA (*grinning*): Tell me, Mrs. Larrabee, have you any more dun-coloured, sallow little mice growing up in odd corners of the property?

MAUDE: Julia, I swear that's the way she was. Wasn't she, David? She *was* shy.

DAVID: Yes, she was. She knew me well because we were the same age, but she was frightened to death of father, and a little of Linus, and she was especially shy with you, because she adored you. You were the Lady in the Picture on the Wall; you were the Fairy Princess. It looks as though you still are.

SABRINA *appears on the terrace, running, dashes down the steps and off to the right, out of sight.*

SABRINA (*as she runs, never stopping*): Excuse me. Margaret wants to see her hat.

JULIA (*after* SABRINA *has gone*): Maude? Whatever vitamin deficiency she may have had as a child has been corrected.

MAUDE: I think it's glandular. And I'd love to know which gland. (*The two women start for the house.*) Do you like her, David?

DAVID: I won't know till she stands still.

MAUDE: I *like* her. And I'd love to know about these past five years in Paris. When a girl blossoms like that, you can be sure there's a man somewhere in the background. Or men.

DAVID (*interested*): Oh?

The women stop to look back.

MAUDE: My! Look at her run!

JULIA: I don't think any man could catch her.
> *She goes in.*

DAVID (*grabbing the cage*): Mother, don't go off without your new friend.

MAUDE: How, David.

DAVID: Come on, mother. You haven't lived until you've been awakened in the morning by a singing cockatoo.

MAUDE (*taking the cage*): I've managed so far. Well . . .
> *She goes into the house, watching the bird warily. A moment, then* SABRINA *runs on, carrying a Paris hat box.* DAVID *manages to be in her way.*

DAVID: Idle down to forty. Your carburettor needs adjusting.

SABRINA (*laughing*): I know. Isn't it terrible? I can't stop. You should have been there at the station when I knocked down father. (*She winces at the memory.*) People picked me up and dusted me off, and I was so rattled, all I could say was: "It's all right, he's my father!" It does sound idiotic, doesn't it? But you know what I meant. It's perfectly permissible to knock down your father, but you never knock down your chauffeur.

DAVID: Oh, I agree! It's one of the first things you learn.

SABRINA (*lovingly*): Ah, David!

DAVID (*smiling down at her*): Glad to be home?

SABRINA (*overflowing*): Oh! ! !

DAVID: You have changed.

SABRINA: It's been a long time, David. Especially for us. Do you know how many years? I was away at college when you went off to the wars, and when you came back, I had gone off to Europe. We're almost strangers.

DAVID: We'll soon fix that.

SABRINA (*with more affection than she would care to know she shows*): You look well, David. And so mature. You're the kind that improves with age.

DAVID: Any grey hairs?

SABRINA (*grinning*): Oh, when you're grey, you'll be irresistible. Isn't it odd, David? We *are* strangers. The only common experience we had was living here and playing together as children, but that's been gone a long time. We've been to opposite ends of the world . . . you've had a war . . . and a marriage . . . and a divorce. . . (*She smiles at him gently.*) I'm sorry about the divorce, David.

DAVID: So am I.

SABRINA: I thought of you on your wedding day. It was a Saturday, and I was in the country, at Saint Germain en Laye, walking down a long *allée* of trees, and I thought:— right now he's walking up the aisle . . . with her.

DAVID: I'm sorry you weren't there.

SABRINA: No, I didn't want to be.

DAVID: Why?

    A small pause.

SABRINA: I liked your wife in the picture I saw. She had . . . distinction. I hoped I would meet her one day.

DAVID: You can; she's here.

SABRINA: Oh, with Linus?

DAVID: Now, how did you know about that?

SABRINA: About Linus and your wife? It's common knowledge.

DAVID: Even in Europe?

SABRINA (*laughing*): Ah, no! But I've been kept informed. I've had a faithful correspondent: Margaret. And I know everything that's happened in this house even to the number of champagne glasses broken last New Year's Eve. I know all about *you*. Every move you've made.

DAVID: Every move?

SABRINA: Almost every move.

DAVID: Margaret must have written very long letters.

SABRINA: She did. I insisted.

    They are smiling at each other with easy familiarity. LINUS *wanders on.*

LINUS: David, you haven't seen a sweater lying around here, have you?

DAVID: A sweater? No.

LINUS: Gretchen thinks she may have left it here. Oh.

He sees the sweater, gets it and starts out. SABRINA *looks up at* DAVID *with a wicked smile of "here I go again", darts over to* LINUS, *and stands before him challengingly.*

SABRINA: Hello.

LINUS: Oh, hello, Sabrina, how are you?

She sucks in for a moment, then, with a small set of the mouth, slams him in the middle with the hat box, turns and darts up the steps and into the house. LINUS *doubles over, soundlessly.* DAVID *collapses with laughter.*

THE CURTAIN FALLS

ACT II

A Friday evening two weeks later. The same walled garden in moonlight. There are areas of shadow that the moon cannot dissipate and that the light from the house cannot quite penetrate. The house is brilliantly lit; there is a party in progress. A four-piece orchestra of that peculiar kind that plays only at house-parties, and that seems always to be playing at a house-party of the twenties, is making its way warily through Gershwin's "Someone to Watch Over Me".

At Rise: MR. LARRABEE *stands on the terrace looking out toward the garden. He wears a dinner jacket and holds a drink in his hand. After a moment, he calls out.*

LARRABEE: Linus? (*He waits, then tries again.*) Linus! (*But obviously his heart is not in it.*)

      MRS. LARRABEE, *in evening dress, appears from the house.*

MAUDE (*anxiously*): Have you found him, Linus?

LARRABEE: No.

MAUDE: Did you look in the bar?

LARRABEE: Yes.

      He takes a drink.

MAUDE: Really it's wrong of him to disappear like this. Poor Mary Townsend looks stricken, and is trying desperately to act as though nothing had happened.

LARRABEE: I can't see that anything very much has happened. You threw a girl at his head and he ducked.

MAUDE: I trust you're not defending your son's manners.

LARRABEE: No, merely his taste. (*He calls.*) Linus?

      JULIA, *in evening dress, comes out of the bar, and the door bangs behind her. She carries a champagne glass, filled to the brim.*

JULIA: He's not in the bar.

MAUDE: Julia, that *is* ginger ale, isn't it?

> JULIA *looks at her warily, examines the drink carefully, then takes a small, tentative sip, and tastes and considers.*

JULIA (*doubtfully*): It's been so long since I *had* ginger ale. . . .

LARRABEE: No reason why she shouldn't have a drink. Alcohol's a preservative.

MAUDE: I don't recall that the doctor said she needed pickling. Do go look for him, Linus.

LARRABEE: Maude, I am too old to be a father. And even at my best, I was not equipped to be Linus' father. You'll excuse me, my dear.

> *He goes into the house, passing two young people who come dancing dreamily out on to the terrace, slowly, their eyes closed.* MAUDE *stares out into the garden grimly, her jaw set.*

JULIA: Give it up. It's not that important.

MAUDE: It is to me.

JULIA: To get Linus married? Why?

MAUDE: I don't want any son of mine to become a lecherous old bachelor.

JULIA: I know a lot of married men who are lecherous old bachelors.

> *With great anticipation she starts to raise the glass to her lips. The dancing couple bumps into her arms; the champagne spills on the ground.*

THE GIRL: Oh!

THE BOY: Oh, I'm terribly sorry!

JULIA (*grimly*): Everybody's against me.

> *She goes back into the bar.*

THE GIRL (*calling*): Did it get on your dress?

MAUDE: No, it didn't ,dear.

THE BOY: I'm sorry, Mrs. Larrabee, we didn't see you.

MAUDE: Perfectly all right, Peter. Dancers have the right of way, this evening. (*She smiles at the girl.*) Are you having a good time?

THE GIRL: Yes, it's a wonderful party.

MAUDE: That's a pretty dress. (*She starts for the house.*)

30

Peter, if you should happen to stroll down to the boathouse, will you look about for Linus? And if you see him, tell him we're about to go in to supper.

THE BOY (*innocently*): Oh, we won't be going down to the boathouse, Mrs. Larrabee. (MAUDE *smiles and goes into the house. The two young people look at each other with slightly lifted eyebrows and slightly challenging smiles, then begin to dance again. They move into an area of shadow, and their movements become smaller and smaller until they are standing still in the archway in the attitude of the dance. Finally they give up all pretence, adjust their arms to a more comfortable position, and lock in a close embrace. Finally, they part.*) Come on.

THE GIRL: Not the boathouse. I'll be cold.

THE BOY: No you won't. Come on.

THE GIRL: No, the boathouse is cold at night.

THE BOY: Well, there's a little house at the end of the rose garden, they call "The Hideaway". Nobody ever goes there. Come on.

> *They hurry off into the garden.* LINUS, *in a dinner jacket, appears in the archway from the other direction, and watches them go with a small smile. The orchestra inside the house stops playing with a small fanfare to indicate that the dancing is ended for the time being, and that supper is about to begin.* LINUS *turns down from the archway, and is about to wander on to the terrace, when he sees someone coming from the direction of the garage. He retires into the shadow of the archway again. A moment, then* SABRINA *appears, and walks on slowly. She wears a simple dress and carries a sweater. She stands quietly looking at the house, then leans on the wall and watches the activity within.*

> *Her father,* FAIRCHILD, *appears from the garage, obviously looking for her. He holds a volume of Everyman's Library, with a finger inserted to hold his place. He looks about, sees her, and moves to her.*

> *From within the house we can hear an accordianist playing modern French waltzes as he wanders through the rooms among the supper guests.*

31

FAIRCHILD: Sabrina. . . . (*She gives the faintest indication that she hears him.*) . . . Sabrina, what are you doing?

SABRINA (*with a small smile*): Watching the rich folk, pappy.

FAIRCHILD: I thought you were going to a movie.

SABRINA: I did. I went into Oyster Bay, and then had a soda at the drug store. Howard Whitman, who want to school with me, was behind the fountain, and he put in an extra scoop of vanilla and asked me if I'd hang around until he knocked off work. I know that song.

FAIRCHILD: Come home, Sabrina. I don't like you doing this.

SABRINA: I always used to do it, father. And it was always such fun. I used to sneak down in my bathrobe and listen to the music and see them all so beautifully dressed. And next day at lunch I had a piece of the cake. Mother saved it for me; and then, after mother died, Margaret saved it for me. But the important thing is that I always had a piece of the cake.

FAIRCHILD (*uncomfortably*): It's different now.

SABRINA: In what way different, father? Margaret will save me a piece of the cake, nothing has changed here.

FAIRCHILD (*accusingly*): *You've* changed!

SABRINA (*flatly*): Well, they're changing me back.

LINUS, *unseen, retires behind the wall of the archway.*

FAIRCHILD: No, not to the way you were. You were such a nice, quiet girl. How could anyone change so much in five years? You were so likeable!

SABRINA: Oh, father! Don't you like me now?

FAIRCHILD (*with a mounting sense of injury*): It's been very unsettling having you home, Sabrina. In just two weeks you've upset everybody: me, Margaret, John, Jessie . . . you have something to say about everything. You want everybody to *do* something. Why should Jessie go to the Metropolitan Museum of Art on her day off? Her feet hurt enough!

SABRINA: I'm sorry! I didn't think of her feet!

FAIRCHILD: Well, you should have!

SABRINA: Yes, I should have. But you needn't fear, father. Paris will wear off. Cinderella's been to her ball, but now she's back in the chimney corner, with no Prince Charming to seek her. (*Ruefully.*) Anyway, I've got such *big* feet.

FAIRCHILD: What's the matter, Sabrina?

SABRINA (*in a burst*): I'd know what to do if they were rude, but I can't cope with being ignored! I just don't know how!

FAIRCHILD: They talked about inviting you. Margaret heard them. I didn't see any reason to tell you. *She* was talking to *him*, and she said she didn't think it would be fair to you to ask you because you'd feel strange among all these people you didn't know.

SABRINA: That was considerate. And what did *he* say?

FAIRCHILD: I don't know.

SABRINA: I can guess. And still I was invited. By David. But then he laughed and said his mother disapproved, and I declined with thanks. (*She smiles at her father.*) Don't worry, father, I didn't embarrass him. I made up a very good excuse that I've forgotten now.

FAIRCHILD (*after a long pause, gently*): Sabrina, I think you ought to go away again.

SABRINA (*far away*): So do I. But where shall I go? I came home from Paris to find out something about myself, and no one's given me a chance to find out. The only thing I've learned is that this isn't home. Where shall it be? Where are my roots? With Howard Whitman and a black and white soda? Or did they go deep in the Faubourg St. Germain des Pres? If I'm a girl without a country? I wouldn't like that to happen to me. (*She looks at the house.*) Do you know? I have an evening dress very much like that——(*She is pointing to the interior of the house and craning her neck.*) My little couturier stole it from Dior. No, mine's twice as smart.

FAIRCHILD: I have some money put away for you, that I was going to give you when you'd settled down. But you can have it now.

SABRINA: Oh, father! I'm a self-supporting woman!

FAIRCHILD: I'd like to give it to you now.

SABRINA: Thank you, father.

FAIRCHILD: You don't ever have to worry about money.

SABRINA: I love you for many things, father, but do you know what I love you for most of all? (*He waits for her to go on.*) That you decided to become a chauffeur because you wanted to have time to read. (*She turns to him and smiles at him brightly, with deep fondness.*) And all my life I've pictured you, sitting in the front seat of that long succession of Cadillacs, waiting for the Larrabee's, and reading. Through the 20's, the 30's and 40's, in rain and snow and hail and sleet, not caring if it was Aristotle or Anthony Hope, so long as it gave you black words on white paper to feed on. How many books is it now, father?

FAIRCHILD: Six thousand, three hundred and twenty-eight.

SABRINA: I am the daughter of a literary tapeworm.

FAIRCHILD: Sabrina,—I like you.

SABRINA: Thank you, father. I want you to.

FAIRCHILD: Come home with me now.

SABRINA: All right. What's that you're reading now?

FAIRCHILD: *Lucretius: The Nature of the Universe.*

SABRINA: Oh, yes. That was required reading in our sophomore year. Much too deep for me. Do you understand it?

FAIRCHILD: No, but I enjoy reading it.

SABRINA: That's fair enough.

> *They go off toward the garage. As they go:*

FAIRCHILD: I've liked my life, Sabrina.

SABRINA: I know. And I'm glad.

> LINUS *comes out from behind the archway and watches them go, thoughtfully. The bar door opens, and* JULIA *appears.*

JULIA: Ah! Home is the hunter. Or is it the sailor? You've been missed. We were about to beat the bushes for you.

LINUS: You overrate me, Aunt Julia. I've got too old for that sort of thing.

JULIA: I've always thought that sort of thing was overrated, anyway.

34

DAVID *appears from the house.*

DAVID: Linus, I've come with a message. Our mother is displeased with you.

LINUS: I am displeased with our mother.

DAVID (*amused*): For the same reason? Mary Townsend? (LINUS *nods.*) You know, in a way this party is for Mary. And for you. Mother has decided Mary is the girl to housebreak you.

LINUS: Mother is wrong.

DAVID: Well, don't take it out on Mary.

LINUS: I have been a devoted partner and a dutiful son. I have dined with Mary, drunk with Mary, and danced with Mary. What more would they have me do with Mary?

JULIA: Your mother worries about you, Linus.

LINUS: I'm sorry for that.

JULIA: And she's begun to wonder at what point an eligible young bachelor becomes a lecherous old bachelor. Have you any views on the subject?

LINUS: I haven't given it much thought. But I'll be glad to ask among my lecherous old friends.

JULIA: You don't think Mary Townsend's the one to save you from that dread fate.

LINUS: No.

DAVID: Mary's a fine girl, Linus.

LINUS: Mary *is* a fine girl. That's why mother shouldn't do this to her.

DAVID: Ah, but Mary likes it. And Mary's mother likes it. And Mary's father thinks you're very sound. Very sound indeed.

LINUS: Mary's father is an ass.

JULIA: Agreed.

DAVID: He's made a lot of money.

LINUS: I know a lot of asses who've made a lot of money. Benjamin Townsend is that particular kind of an ass who thinks making money is a holy rite of which he is the anointed high priest. If he should ever discover it's a small knack, like juggling three oranges, he'd fall apart.

(*He almost growls.*) If making money were all there was to business, it would hardly be worth going to the office once a week. Money's a by-product.

DAVID: But such an attractive by-product.

JULIA (*staring at* LINUS *thoughtfully*): What's the main object in view, Linus? Power?

LINUS (*after a moment*): That's become a dirty word.

JULIA: Most of the strong words have.

> *He meets her challenging gaze steadfastly. Finally:*

LINUS: Control.

> *She nods.*

DAVID: Well, you've got quite a bit of that. You are Larrabee Industries. Still, marrying Mary would give you a bit more. There's Townsends Steel and Townsends Sulphur . . .

JULIA: The bride wore a satin gown edged with old common and preferred stock.

LINUS (*lightly, but deeply serious underneath*): If I should ever decide I wanted control of Townsend Steel and Townsend Sulphur, I'd like to think I could get it without prostituting the Townsend daughter.

DAVID: That's a noble thought.

LINUS: Or myself.

JULIA: That's an afterthought. Be careful of those better instincts, Linus. They don't go with your reputation. (*She moves to the house.*) Shall I check you in?

LINUS: I'd rather you didn't.

JULIA: You're still in the bushes. (*A moment.*) Linus? (*He looks at her.*) If I were thirty years younger, you wouldn't have a chance.

LINUS: I wouldn't put up a struggle.

> *She raises her glass to him, and goes in.*

DAVID: You'd better come along in.

LINUS: Not yet.

DAVID: I'll protect you.

LINUS: It's time we stirred things up, David. Serenity can be damned dull.

DAVID: Not for me. The quiet life for me.

A YOUNG MAN *and a* YOUNG LADY *have eased out of the house rather carefully, and now work above them and make a break for the gardens.* LINUS *catches sight of them.*

LINUS: Hello!

They stop short.

THE YOUNG MAN: Oh, hello, Linus, David. Going in to supper?

LINUS: Is it worth it?

YOUNG MAN: Yes, it's quite a spread. Betty has a headache. We thought we'd stroll down to the boathouse. Get some air.

LINUS: You'll find the boathouse pretty cold.

THE YOUNG WOMAN: We weren't going to stay there!

LINUS: Have you ever seen mother's rose garden? It's quite beautiful in the moonlight. It's on the second terrace down, with a stone fountain, and a little house at the end we call "The Hideaway".

Pause.

THE YOUNG WOMAN: I like roses.

THE YOUNG MAN: Yes, that sounds nice. We'll take a look. Thanks, Linus.

They start off quite casually.

LINUS: Glad to be of assistance.

They glance over their shoulders once, then disappear.

DAVID: What was that for?

LINUS: A small experiment in traffic management. Shouldn't you be doing that sort of thing?

DAVID (*grinning*): Give me time. The evening's young. (*Pause.* DAVID *hesitates, then decides to say it.*) Linus . . . what's become of my dear ex-wife, Gretchen?

LINUS *turns his head and looks at him reflectively.*

LINUS: You didn't like that, did you?

DAVID: It wasn't the best joke in the world.

LINUS: I'm sorry. It seemed funny at the time. But the joke wore thin.

DAVID: Did you drop her?

37   D

LINUS: We came to an understanding. That we had no understanding.

DAVID: Good enough. She had it coming.

And then he looks up and smiles apologetically for having said it.

LINUS: And still you miss being married, don't you?

DAVID: I never was married, really. But I'd like to be. I miss being in love.

LINUS: It's such a drain on the resources, David. It leaves so little time for anything else.

DAVID: Are you sure the things you occupy yourself with are that much more important? I'd like to prove to myself that marriage can be a pretty good occupation.

LINUS (*with an approving smile*): Then we'll have to put you to work. Go find yourself a girl.

DAVID: Okay. (*He moves toward the door.*) Will you come in soon? (LINUS *nods.*) *Make* it soon, will you?

He raises his hand in a small, affectionate gesture, and goes in. Long pause. LINUS *wanders up the terrace, and is about to light a cigarette, when he sees someone coming from the garage. He flicks out the match and steps into shadow.* SABRINA *appears, takes her sweater from the wall where she left it, glances at the house and turns back toward the garage.*

LINUS: Hello, Sabrina.

She turns back.

SABRINA: Oh, hello.

And at that moment, the female member of the first amorous couple we saw comes stalking through the opening in the garden wall and heads for the house grimly. She is followed in a moment by her confused and slightly dishevelled young man, who is trying to fix his tie as he hurries after her. No sooner have they disappeared into the house, when the girl of the second couple appears from the garden and heads for the bar. Her young man is right behind her, and still eager.

THE YOUNG MAN: But it's all right! They're gone!

THE YOUNG WOMAN: Oh, shut up!

They go into the bar.

LINUS: My, they look mad, don't they? I wonder why.

SABRINA (*amused*): Where do you suppose it was? At "The Hideaway"?

LINUS: I imagine so. Ever been there?

SABRINA: Oh, yes. But never at night. And never . . . (*And with that "And never", she comes back to where she'd been, and assumes a quiet formality. He waits. Then she speaks matter-of-factly, with no sense of apology or self-consciousness.*) I came out for a breath of air.

LINUS: So did I.

    Pause.

SABRINA: Good night.

LINUS: Good night. (*She turns and goes. He watches until she is well across. Then:*) Do you still have a scar on your right leg? (*She stops and turns and stares at him, startled.*)

SABRINA: Yes.

LINUS (*nods dismissal*): Good night.

SABRINA: Good night. (*She turns again and goes off. He waits. She reappears.*) How did you know about that scar on my leg?

LINUS: I put it there.

SABRINA: When?

LINUS: A long time ago. I came running across there from around back of the garage, and didn't see you, and knocked you crashing into that trellis. You don't remember.

SABRINA: No.

LINUS: You were a very little girl. I picked you up and set you there on the wall, and tried to get you to stop crying. But you wouldn't stop. And when I set you down, you ran away.

SABRINA: Oh. (*She considers, then smiles.*) I think that deep Freudian wound should have healed by now.

LINUS: I hope so. I washed the other one off with cold water.

SABRINA: Thank you. (*Pause.*) I'm sorry I hit you in the stomach with the hat box.

LINUS: It was rather familiar.

39

SABRINA: Well, for someone who knows where that scar is because he put it there. . . . Still, we never did know each other, did we?

LINUS: And there's not much we can do about it, at this distance.

SABRINA: No. (*She comes to him slowly and stands before him.*) Ten years difference in age is a large gap, isn't it?

LINUS: Only among children.

SABRINA: What would you like to know?

LINUS: How you like being home.

SABRINA: It's . . . interesting.

LINUS: And what you've done these past two weeks.

SABRINA: Wandered about New York, mostly. I don't really know New York. That's been fun.

LINUS: You should have called me when you were in town. I'd have taken you to lunch.

SABRINA: I hardly know you. (*He acknowledges that one.*) But David's taken me to lunch. He's been sweet.

LINUS: And how did you like Paris.

SABRINA: Very much. Oh, very much.

LINUS: Was the job interesting?

SABRINA: Yes. Especially towards the end.

LINUS: Were you good at it?

SABRINA: I was very good at it. I went from file clerk to secretary to private secretary, and ended with a secretary of my own. I was quick, bright, and efficient.

LINUS: Sterling qualities in a woman.

SABRINA: Oh?

LINUS: But I can see you have others.

SABRINA: It sounds as through you were interviewing me for a job.

LINUS: Maybe I am.

SABRINA: Thank you, I'm not looking for a job.

LINUS: Who were you private secretary to?

SABRINA (*reciting, with a smile*): Assistant Economic Commissioner Office of Special Representative for Europe Economic Co-operation Administration. Paris.

LINUS: France?

SABRINA: For security reasons we cannot give out that information.

They grin at each other.

LINUS: Will you do something for me?

SABRINA: What?

He takes her by the elbow and conducts her to the wall. There he turns her with her back to the wall, and puts his hands under her elbows.

LINUS: Up!!

He lifts her to a seat on the wall.

SABRINA (*smiling*): I may burst out crying again.

LINUS: That's what I want to see.

SABRINA (*with a look of surprise*): I almost could! I wonder why?

LINUS: You're still a little girl. (*A moment, then:*) How did you get your name?

SABRINA: Sabrina? From father's reading, of course. He was struggling through Milton's *Comus* when I was born . . .

She quotes:

"Sabrina fair
    Listen where thou art sitting
    Under the glassy, cool, translucent wave
    In twisted braids of lilies knitting
    The loose train of thy amber-dropping hair."

Poor father. He got fooled.

LINUS: And what does it mean?

SABRINA: In one sentence, so that he who does not wish to read may run, it is the story of a water nymph who saves a virgin from a fate worse than death.

LINUS: Is Sabrina the virgin?

SABRINA: Sabrina is the saviour.

Pause.

LINUS (*abruptly*): Why did you run away from Paris?

SABRINA (*ruefully*): That was a good guess. I don't see how a thing like that could show.

LINUS: Was it because you were in love with him, or because you weren't?

SABRINA: Are you always so . . . perceptive?

LINUS: Only in business dealings.

SABRINA: Is this business?

LINUS: You may have something I want.

SABRINA: I hardly think so. Good night.

> *She braces with her hands to spring down from the wall, but he is in her way and she cannot.*

LINUS: You're too little a girl to jump to such big conclusions. Is he French or is he American, and did you run away because he wants to marry you or because he doesn't?

SABRINA (*her eyes narrow, and she speaks in cold anger, precisely*): He is French. He wishes to marry me. You are being presumptuous in a way you wouldn't be with anyone else, and I don't like it. Good night. (*She gives him a sharp push away and jumps down and starts for the garage. Unfortunately, however, having had the last word, she can't help adding another over her shoulder.*) And he's extremely rich!

LINUS (*delighted*): Why, you little snob!

> SABRINA *stops and turns, amazed.*

SABRINA (*outraged*): Me?

LINUS: Yes, you! Did you think you could impress me with the fact that a rich Frenchman wants to marry you? How rich is he? Is he richer than I am?

SABRINA (*sadly*): Oh. I didn't mean it that way.

LINUS: Yes, you did. And quite right, too. The rich are impressed by money; they have to be.

SABRINA: You're not.

LINUS: Some are contemptuous of money; they can afford to be. Will you come back to your wall?

SABRINA: No.

LINUS: You may as well tell me about it. You have no one else to tell.

SABRINA: That's not true!

LINUS: Besides, it's sometimes better to tell these things to . . . a stranger.

And at this she must smile broadly, and he takes advantage of the smile to move to her and lead her to a nearby table. He takes her firmly by the elbows and sets her up on the table.

SABRINA (*very much the little girl, wailing*): Why do I have to perch?

LINUS: It lets me feel that I have you.

SABRINA: I don't want you to feel that you have me!

LINUS: You must tell me everything, my child.

SABRINA: I don't like the sound of that, either! Why isn't there any music?

LINUS: They've gone in to supper. Would you like a drink?

SABRINA: Yes!

LINUS: I'll get you one in a minute. Is he madly in love with you?

SABRINA: Yes!

LINUS: Are you madly in love with him?

SABRINA: No! But I'm madly in love with the life he offers. And that's the trouble.

LINUS: Loads of money and a house in Paris.

SABRINA: *And* a house in Burgundy, with a vineyard! A *real* vineyard that makes one of the very *best* burgundies!

LINUS: That *is* an attraction! And a good Burgundian cook to go with it?

SABRINA: Oh, a fantastic cook! I can't tell you! The most amazing food you've ever tasted!

LINUS: You must ask me down. What else?

SABRINA: The south of France when it's gay, and London once a year; and skiing at Chamonix, or in Switzerland at Davos, or in Austria—and oh! shooting! He loves to shoot and he's a wonderful shot, and the woods are so lovely in autumn. (*Like a little girl showing off, proudly.*) Wild boar.

LINUS (*fascinated*): Eh?

SABRINA (*proudly*): He shoots wild boar in Belgium.

LINUS: I'll marry him myself.

Which breaks it for SABRINA, *and she laughs aloud.*

SABRINA: Don't be fooled; he's not a playboy. He works hard.

LINDUS: At what?

SABRINA: Stocks and bonds and industries and things. You know:—deals. He goes to Switzerland a lot.

LINUS: On skis?

SABRINA: Oh, really!

LINUS: What's his name?

SABRINA: I won't tell you.

LINUS: I think you've made him up.

SABRINA: I have not! He's five-feet-eleven and weighs a hundred and sixty pounds and wears glasses, and has a lovely moustache.

LINUS: Sounds like the entire French Chamber of Deputies.

SABRINA: He's a very distinguished person!

LINUS: He offers you a great deal, Sabrina.

SABRINA (*softly, glowing*): I know. The house in Paris is lovely . . . and all the things that go with it; the people and the places; the clothes and the jewels. . . (*She chuckles softly.*) I would even have a car and chauffeur of my own.

LINUS: Is that your private little joke, or does he share it?
Her eyes narrow a little, and she smiles frostily.

SABRINA (*with spaced precision*): He calls me: "*sa petite fille du chauffeur*", which, in your schoolboy French, may be translated as: "his little daughter of the chauffeur."

LINUS: A term of endearment, I take it, like: "my little cabbage."

SABRINA: Exactly.

LINUS: I apologise.

SABRINA: You should.

LINUS: Why don't you marry him?
Pause.

SABRINA: I'm afraid.

LINUS: Of what?

SABRINA: Of being domesticated. (*He laughs.*) That's not funny. Do you think men have the exclusive right to run from domestication? Pooh! That's a myth! Men adore it!

LINUS: You've found that out.

SABRINA: Yes.

LINUS: And you want no part of domesticity.

SABRINA: I didn't say that. I love being domestic. I'm afraid of being domesticated. There's a difference.

LINUS (*impressed*): Ah, you've found that out, too.

SABRINA: Do you understand that?

LINUS (*almost grimly*): Yes. I do.

SABRINA: The trouble with marriage is that men want to give you the world, but it has to be the world they want to give you. And what of the other worlds outside the window? Do you know what I mean? The things he does are fun to do, and I love doing them with him, and you can't have a marriage without that. But suppose then I find that they keep me from doing all the other wonderful things I've wanted to do? Suppose I find that instead of opening up my life, I've closed it down and locked it off?

LINUS: You can't do everything, Sabrina.

SABRINA: Ah, but it's important to try!

LINUS: What do you want to do, Sabrina?

SABRINA: I don't know.

LINUS: What *can* you do?

SABRINA: Nothing impressive. (*Musically, thinking aloud.*) I cannot sing a song or write a poem or paint a picture, and I shall never run for Senator from Connecticut——

LINUS: Why Connecticut?

SABRINA: It makes a nice sound.

LINUS: That's as good a reason for running as any.

SABRINA: But I think I have a talent, all the same. I think I have a talent for living. Perhaps I'm trying to make the most of something small for want of something better, but I think a true talent for living has the quality of creation, and if that's the talent I was meant to have, I'm awfully glad I have it. I'd rather live a first-rate life than paint a second-rate picture.

LINUS *is gently amused at this self-dramatisation.*

LINUS: So would a lot of second-rate painters. Do you know how to live a first-rate life?

SABRINA: I'm beginning to learn; I've been to school.

LINUS: In Paris. (*She nods.*) And what did Paris teach you?

SABRINA (*proudly*): Two things! To develop my appetites; and to discipline them.

LINUS: That's admirable.

SABRINA: And to want to do everything and see everything, sense everything and feel everything and taste everything; to know that life is an enormous experience and must be used. To be in the world, and of the world, and never to stand aside and watch.

LINUS: You never learned that in Paris.

SABRINA: Where, then?

LINUS: It sounds more like Ralph Waldo Emerson.

SABRINA: You mustn't laugh at me.

LINUS: I could hardly laugh at such an impressive mixture of high principles and higher living. Sabrina, how would you like to be a Joan of Arc, and march at the head of a devout company of transcendental epicureans? Whose aim shall be: a bottle of the best burgundy on every table; a tin of *pâté de fois gras* on every shelf? And whose motto, inscribed on the banner you carry, shall be——

SABRINA: What?

LINUS: What else? "Let them eat cake!"

SABRINA (*laughing*): Oh, I like that! But you are laughing at me, and you shouldn't.

LINUS: I can't help it. You have another talent, Sabrina: a talent for making me laugh. Paris has gone to your head, Sabrina. You've learned too much too fast, and your worldliness is a little soft around the edges.

SABRINA: Oh. The day I came home. (*She winces slightly, thinking of it.*) The cockatoo was not a success, was it? (*He shakes his head.*) It seemed such a nice idea at the time.

LINUS: It was a romantic idea, as most of your ideas seem to be. Shall I teach you to be realistic?

SABRINA: Do you think you can?

LINUS (*deadly serious*): In one easy lesson. Marry your Frenchman. You'll never have it so good again. (*She stares at
him anxiously.*) Have no qualms, Sabrina. Marrying for
love is a romantic American idea.

SABRINA (*hopefully*): I'm fond of him.

LINUS: Do you love someone else?

SABRINA: I'm not sure. There's someone I think I've been
in love with all my life, but since it goes way back, it may
not be real, now. I've never had a chance to find out.

LINUS: Don't bother to find out. Marry your Frenchman.

SABRINA: Oh, no! I must find out!

LINUS: Would it do you any good if you did?

SABRINA: I don't think so.

LINUS: Then don't bother.

SABRINA: That's not the kind of advice you give yourself.
You seem to be spending your life finding out.

LINUS: We're looking for different things. I've shot wild
boar in Belgium.

SABRINA: You have?

LINUS: Marry your Frenchman, Sabrina. Don't compare
yourself to me. I've already got a chauffeur.

SABRINA: That was rude.

LINUS (*grimly*): How to be realistic in one easy lesson.

SABRINA: I want to find out!

LINUS: Who is this you think you're in love with?

    DAVID *appears from the house.*

DAVID: Hey, Linus!

SABRINA (*startled*): Oh!

LINUS (*just as startled, when he sees her reaction*): David? Is it
David?

SABRINA (*in confusion*): Ah!

    DAVID *has run down the steps and crossed to them.*

DAVID (*grimly, to* LINUS): Now you *are* being rude.

LINUS: Oh. Mary. Yes, I guess I am. (*He is tense with delight
and excitement*): Sabrina wants a drink. I was just about
to get it for her.

DAVID: I'll get it. What would you like, Sabrina?

SABRINA: Scotch, please. With soda, lots of soda.

DAVID *starts for the bar.* LINUS *stops to move a chair.*

LINUS: What's Mary doing?

DAVID: Sitting in the living room with Harry Selby, explaining how they make steel.

DAVID *goes into the bar. As soon as he is gone,* LINUS *speeds back to* SABRINA *and leans across the table to her with eager delight.*

LINUS: It *is* David, isn't it?

SABRINA (*defiantly*): No!

LINUS: It has to be! Someone you've known all your life! It couldn't be anyone else!

SABRINA: Just because I was brought up there over the garage doesn't mean I was cloistered!

LINUS: Don't tell me it's Howard Whitman who went to school with you and now jerks sodas in Oyster Bay?

SABRINA: How did you know about *him*?

LINUS: You have no secrets from me, Sabrina.

SABRINA: It might be someone I met at college!

LINUS: You went to a women's college!

SABRINA: We sometimes imported men!

LINUS: Sabrina, be honest! It's David! Do you want him? You can have him!

SABRINA: Don't say that!

LINUS: Why not? (*He is in a fever of intense delight.*) Oh, this is better than the Frenchman! You've developed expensive tastes in men, Sabrina. But David's the one to give you the world. Even the most bountiful of Frenchmen are careful. Take David, Sabrina. David's the one!

SABRINA (*frightened*): You make it sound like a game!

LINUS (*savagely*): It is a game! The most exciting game in the world! With life-size figures! Who shall capture whom, and who shall capture the world!

SABRINA: What about love?

LINUS (*with contemptuous assurance*): What *about* love? Love is the measure of defeat. The one who loves is captured.

SABRINA (*unequal to this struggle*): Ah, no!

48

LINUS: Must you have it with love? Then remember, Sabrina, you left someone behind in Paris and came three thousand miles because you've loved David all your life!

SABRINA: No, to find out!

LINUS: And you'd be so good for David! You're what David needs! All you have to do is tell him you've always loved him . . . and he'll fall like a peach. Think of it, Sabrina! All your dreams come true, and twice over! Two men, and yours for the taking! *You* have the power of choice! You! *"la petite fille du chauffeur"*—*you* are in the driver's seat! (*And with that, he thinks he hears* DAVID *coming, and races across and up the steps and stops in the doorway of the house to face across to* SABRINA. *The bar door opens, and* DAVID *appears, holding two highballs.* LINUS *raises an admonishing finger.*) Take him!

He runs into the house. SABRINA *stares after him, rigid with anxiety.*

THE CURTAIN FALLS

ACT III

The following morning MARGARET, *the maid, is clearing breakfast dishes from a table in the walled garden and is placing them on a tray. It is late in the morning; the sun is high.* LINUS *appears on the terrace in the same old sailing clothes he wore when we first met him. He wanders to the edge of the terrace. He carries a small leather volume of verse.*

LINUS: Margaret, have you seen Mr. David?

MARGARET: It's his breakfast dishes I'm clearing away, sir. And that late, he'll not eat a bite of lunch.

LINUS: Where's he gone?

MARGARET: He's walking in the garden with your mother.

> *He glances to the north, but does not see them. He walks down the steps, then stops, irresolutely. He looks off to the garage, sees nothing, and turns his attention to the transfer of plates from table to tray.*

LINUS (*after a while*): I don't suppose you've seen Sabrina this morning.

MARGARET: Sabrina? Yes, sir. She's up there on the balcony, sunning herself.

> LINUS, *surprised, looks over at the garage, sees something, and is quite puzzled.*

LINUS: Where's her face?

MARGARET (*amused*): It's her hair that's covering it, sir: she's drying her hair.

> *He nods, accepting the explanation as rational, and moves across to call.*

LINUS (*calling*): Sabrina?

SABRINA (*from off stage*): What? Oh! Good morning, Linus! (*Her voice is bright and gay.*) I thought of something last night, much later, and I've been saving it for you! If I'm Joan of Arc, then you must be Alexander the Great! (*He winces and glances at* MARGARET, *who has stopped work at this, and is staring at him. He looks back to* SABRINA, *who takes that as her cue to explain.*) Weeping for new worlds to conquer! (*He winces again, terribly.*)

LINUS: Come down here. I want to talk to you.

SABRINA: What?

LINUS: Come down here!

SABRINA: I can't! I've just washed my hair!

LINUS: That doesn't matter.

SABRINA: Yes, it does! When a girl washes her hair, she takes off all her clothes! At least, I do!

LINUS: I want to talk to you!

SABRINA: What about? (*He makes no answer.*) Is someone there? Oh! Margaret, you mustn't listen! This is a private conversation!

MARGARET (*bristling with indignation, but more to herself than to* SABRINA): I'm sure I have no interest in anything you have to say, young lady.

    And with great bustle, she moves the tray and scrubs the table.

SABRINA: Isn't it a beautiful morning, Linus? The minute I woke up and looked out the window, I knew I would have to wash my hair!

LINUS (*imperatively*): Sabrina!

SABRINA (*with mocking gaiety*): Yes, Linus! I found out!

    He makes a move in her direction, but stops short as he sees her go into her room. We hear the screen door slam. He stares after her in exasperated amusement.

    JULIA *appears on the terrace, carrying a cup of coffee.*

LINUS: She seems happy, Margaret.

MARGARET: She was always a happy child, sir.

    She picks up the tray and starts for the house.

LINUS: Bring me some coffee, will you please?

MARGARET: Yes, sir.

    She goes into the house.

JULIA (*sitting down, shakily*): I'll be honest: I have a teentsy-weentsy hangover. From one half, of one glass, of champagne. (*She quotes, with some distate.*) "Grow old along

with me. . . . The best is yet to be." . . . Robert Browning
was a damned fool.

LINUS: Aunt Julia. . . .

JULIA: Hmmm?

LINUS: A young lady awakens in the morning, looks out
the window, and decides to wash her hair. What does it
mean?

JULIA: Linus, I'm not up to playing games this morning.

LINUS: Would it mean that something particularly nice has
happened to her?

JULIA: It quite often does. More often, it means that her
hair needs washing. Anybody I know?

LINUS: When are you going to let me take you sailing, Aunt
Julia?

JULIA: I could never see the charm in getting wet at a forty-
five degree angle. You're looking terribly pleased with
yourself, this morning.

LINUS: Yes, I feel quite god-like this morning.

JULIA: There's no use asking why.

LINUS: Not at this point in the game.

JULIA: What game?

LINUS: Have you ever shot wild boar in Belgium, Aunt
Julia? (*She winces; her head does ache.*) We must have David
take it up.

JULIA: Linus, there are times when your way of saying and
doing the unexpected has a certain charm. But not this
morning.

LINUS (*cheerfully*): My only pleasure in life is doing the unexpected. It has made me greatly admired in business, and
greatly frowned on in society.

> JULIA *opens her eyes and fixes him with a direct look.*

JULIA: I think you thought that up, one day, and wrote it
down.

LINUS (*grinning*): Why, Aunt Julia!

> MAUDE *and* DAVID *appear from the garden, deep in
> conversation.* MAUDE *looks exasperated;* DAVID *has a set
> smile.*

DAVID: . . . after all, I'm not a child.

MAUDE: No, David, I *am* surprised at your attitude. There's no earthly reason why you should have a chip on your shoulder. Really!

DAVID: Obviously I'm going to have trouble with my family.

MAUDE: Not at all! But you certainly owe it to us to sit down and discuss the matter quietly—— (*She becomes aware of* LINUS *and* JULIA.) Oh.

LINUS: What happened to you last night, David? You suddenly disappeared.

DAVID: I went sailing.

LINUS: At midnight?

DAVID: There was a wonderful, lop-sided moon. . . .

LINUS: Yes, there was, wasn't there? But I don't remember that there was anyone at the party worth sharing it with.

DAVID: There wasn't. At the party.

MAUDE: Linus: David wants to marry Sabrina. You know— (*She waves at the garage.* LINUS *sucks in his breath, and his eyes widen with suppressed pleasure and triumph.* JULIA *stares at him.*) Julia, we've agreed not so say anything for a while——

DAVID: (*impatiently*): Now, mother!

MAUDE: Well, Linus?

LINUS *exhales, and grins at* DAVID.

LINUS: Congratulations.

MAUDE: Oh.

DAVID (*gratefully*): Thank you, Linus.

MAUDE: There! You see, David? No one in the family is going to be against you. We can all understand your falling in love with the girl. But are you sure you want to marry her?

DAVID: Mother, we've been through all that. And I resent your putting Sabrina in the category of——

MAUDE: I'm not putting her in any category, David. I'm very fond of the girl, but——

LINUS: Mother, if you don't mind, I'd like to know how it happened. What's the story, David?

DAVID: You were here. Remember? I brought her a drink, and we talked for a while, and then we decided to go out on the water. We didn't sail; I took the cruiser. The wind was dropping and I was afraid of the tide. (LINUS *nods agreement*.) And that's all. We wandered about the Sound all night, and talked.

MAUDE: That's exactly what I mean. How can you know you want to marry a girl, after spending one night out on the Sound talking to her?

LINUS: What would you have suggested he do with her? (*His mother fixes him icily*.) Sorry, mother.

DAVID (*with a regretful smile*): As to that, I tried that, too, but she wouldn't let me.

JULIA: Good for her.

MAUDE: Yes, that was clever of her.

JULIA: Ooh!!

LINUS *gives a sharp whoop of laughter*.

DAVID: Mother!

MAUDE: Careful! (*This last is at sight of MARGARET, who appears on the terrace carrying a small silver tray with coffee service for one. They turn and watch her approach and set the tray on the table. But the silence becomes intolerable for MAUDE, who was brought up always to fill gaps in the conversation. She speaks up, a bit too brightly*.) Margaret, did I tell you to set another place for lunch?

MARGARET: Yes, madam.

MAUDE: Thank you. (*MARGARET goes on toward the house, and MAUDE now has something to talk about*.) I had the most amusing conversation on the phone yesterday afternoon. It was a man calling from New York to say he had just arrived from Paris and was stopping at the St. Regis and had a note of introduction to me from Madge de Lessac, and could he deliver it in person. He sounded so charming, I took a chance and asked him out to lunch. I'm sure Madge wouldn't send me anyone who——(*MARGARET is gone. MAUDE takes a deep breath*.) Now, David! I don't want to continue this discussion until after I've talked to

54

your father. But I want you to believe something. Will you? I want you to believe that I am on your side. (*And now, at her most wide-eyed.*) Oh, how could you ever dream that I would be against anything you wanted, unless I thought it was wrong for you? You remember, dear, I was never very happy about Gretchen.

DAVID (*uncomfortably*): Yes, mother, I remember. And this is different.

MAUDE: Of course it's different! (*And then:*) Are you sure it's different, David?

DAVID: Yes.

MAUDE (*softly*): You wanted Gretchen just as much. It may not be different, David.

DAVID: Yes, this girl is different from any girl I've ever known. (*To* LINUS.) You remember what I said to you last night. (LINUS *nods.*) There she was, all the time. It didn't take long to find out. When you're with Sabrina, you find yourself suddenly talking about things you've always wanted to do and that you've forgotten. You become aware of all the things you've missed and all the things you're missing. She's so much in love with life, there's so much of the feeling of life in her, that you want to take hold, you want to have her, because maybe if you do, you'll have what she has. I know it sounds . . . young. But when you're with her, that's how you feel.

MAUDE (*softly, smiling, almost weeping for his innocence*): Ah, David . . . don't you know that if there were anyone like that in the world, I would turn the world over to get her for you?

DAVID (*with a soft smile*): There she is, mother.

MAUDE: You're my sweet, idiot child. Linus, will you tell him?

LINUS (*stolidly*): Tell him what, mother?

She stares at him, then at DAVID, *and decides she can say no more.*

MAUDE: Very well, I'll talk to your father. He's gone to a funeral; he should be in a good humour. And no matter what happens, I expect all of you to be full of bright chit-chat at lunch. *Damn* Madge de Lessac! *I* would never plop someone down on *her* out of a clear sky and say, "Have him for lunch." Oh! Fairchild. (FAIRCHILD *has appeared at left.*) Is the funeral over? Already?

FAIRCHILD: Yes, madam. Jessie said you wanted to see me.

MAUDE: No, I—— oh. Yes, I wanted you to meet someone at the station, but I decided you wouldn't be back in time, so I sent John. (*She stares at him, thinking there should be something more to say, then gives up.*) Thank you, Fairchild.

    He nods and goes. She stares after him.

DAVID (*with a small smile*): I know what you're thinking, mother.

MAUDE: He's a very sweet man. And very well read. Go find your father. (DAVID *starts for the house.*) And David. Not a word.

DAVID: No.

    He goes. MAUDE *looks at* LINUS *grimly.*

MAUDE: Linus, go away.

LINUS: I'd enjoy staying, mother.

MAUDE: I know you'd enjoy staying. That's why I want you to go.

    He rises, holding the book of verse, and wanders over in her direction.

LINUS: Mother, did you know that Sabrina's name comes from Milton's "The Masque of Comus"? I wonder if David knows this passage. (*He reads.*)

        "Whilst from off the waters fleet
        Thus I set my printless feet
        Gentle swain, at thy request, I am here."

    He grins down at his mother.

MAUDE (*sharply*): Will you please go.

    He smiles and starts for the garden.

JULIA: Linus, did Sabrina wash her hair this morning?

LINUS: I believe she did, Aunt Julia. I'm thinking of washing mine.

    He goes.

MAUDE: What was that about?

JULIA: I don't know. But I'd like to.

MAUDE: I should have known I was going to have trouble with that girl, the minute she gave me that bird. Ah, my poor, sweet David. A sitting duck if ever there was one.

JULIA: I don't think she's that kind of a girl, Maude.

MAUDE: Don't be silly. Every girl is that kind of a girl. She got a taste of high life in Paris, and decided she'd look for more of it at home. She certainly didn't have to look far. She moved right in with two Cadillacs and a Ford.

JULIA: Maude, I have a feeling about this girl——

MAUDE: And we don't know *any*thing about what she did in Paris!

JULIA: I believe she worked for the United States Government.

MAUDE: You know very well what I mean. No girl moves in the circles she did, and gets to know the people she knew, by being an excellent typist.

LARRABEE *appears on the terrace.*

LARRABEE: Good morning, Julia.

JULIA: Good morning. Did you have fun?

LARRABEE (*to* MAUDE): David said you wanted to see me.

MAUDE: Yes. (*Hopefully.*) Was it a nice funeral, Linus?

LARRABEE: It was a wretched funeral.

MAUDE: Oh.

LARRABEE: People should be horsewhipped for such bungling It started late, ended early, and from beginning to end, no one seemed to know what he was doing. I never saw such shilly-shallying.

JULIA: But they did get the coffin into the grave.

LARRABEE: Since I was not allowed to attend the interment, I couldn't say. But I'd give two to one against.

MAUDE: Oh, that is too bad. But I suppose the poor things just didn't have time to plan. It *was* an unexpected death, wasn't it?

LARRABEE: How can death be unexpected?

 He opens a cigarette box, examines the contents, then tries another.

JULIA: Maude, do you think a poor, tired old invalid could have her lunch peacefully upstairs on a tray?

MAUDE: Traitor.

JULIA (*with a sweet smile*): Thank you.

 She goes into the house.

LARRABEE: Are there no cigarettes of mine out here?

MAUDE (*looking in the box he's looked in*): I'm afraid not, dear.

LARRABEE: Never mind.

 He gets out a gold case, takes a cigarette, and settles himself as MAUDE *watches.*

MAUDE (*finally*): We're having a guest for lunch. A friend of Madge de Lessac's, from Paris.

LARRABEE: Is that what you wanted to tell me?

MAUDE: Well, no. I'm sorry you had a bad morning, dear.

LARRABEE: It wasn't completely wasted. They had a rather good hymn that was new to me. I may use it for myself.

MAUDE: That's good.

LARRABEE: I wrote down the number.

 He begins to hum, trying to remember the tune, but has to give it up as a bad job.

MAUDE: Linus. . . . David came and talked to me this morning.

LARRABEE: Yes? What about?

MAUDE: He thinks he wants to get married again.

LARRABEE (*in good humour, now*): Resilient, isn't he? Who is it this time? One of those young things he was dancing with last night?

MAUDE: Well, he didn't dance with her. (*Thoughtfully.*) I wonder if it was my fault. It may easily have been, now that I think of it. It may never have happened if I had let David ask her to the party.

 She thinks about that.

LARRABEE (*after a pause*): Hmmm?

MAUDE: Hell hath no fury like a woman scorned, you know.

LARRABEE: So I've always been given to understand. I doubt if it's been verified. Who is it that was scorned?

MAUDE: Sabrina. We didn't ask her to the party.

LARRABEE: Who's Sabrina?

MAUDE: Sabrina Fairchild. Fairchild's daughter.

LARRABEE (*remembering*): Oh! Oh, oh, oh! Sabrina! Did she expect to be invited?

MAUDE: Linus, don't you remember? We talked about it.

LARRABEE: Oh, yes.

MAUDE: And I'm sure she wanted to be.

LARRABEE: Well, that's nonsense. But I was quite taken with that girl. I have a feeling she's going to get somewhere.

MAUDE: She already has.

LARRABEE: Hmmm? Well, let's not get off the subject. Who is it David wants to marry?

MAUDE: Sabrina.

LARRABEE: Who?

MAUDE (*exasperated*): Oh, Linus, I get so tired of repeating things! Sabrina! Sabrina Fairchild! Your chauffeur's daughter!

LARRABEE (*after a moment*): You needn't have put it so bluntly. Where is David?

> *That last almost ominously.*

MAUDE: Now, Linus, we must discuss this calmly.

LARRABEE (*with murderous calm*): I see no reason why it should be discussed at all. (*Calling.*) David!

MAUDE: I'm sorry I put it that way; I didn't intend to. The fact that she's your chauffeur's daughter doesn't really matter, Linus. People don't care about that sort of thing any more.

LARRABEE: I. . . . DO! *David!*

MAUDE: But Linus, remember: we're living in the twentieth century!

> *He turns and looks at her as though she had gone mad, and then speaks with controlled force.*

LARRABEE: I have lived in the twentieth century for over fifty years, which is as long as any man has lived in the twentieth century, and longer than most. And I feel I know as much about it as the next man. Just what has the twentieth century to do with my son wanting to marry that girl?

MAUDE: Now, gently, Linus. And don't you dare shout at David.

LARRABEE (*going on as though he hadn't heard her*): If the twentieth century encourages that sort of thing and that sort of thinking, then it's a damned silly century, and the sooner we get out of it, the better. (*With quiet loathing.*) The twentieth century! I could pick a century blindfolded out of a hat and get a better one! (DAVID *appears on the terrace.*) Would you mind coming down, please? (DAVID *descends the steps and approaches.*) You may go, Maude.

MAUDE (*with fire*): I certainly will not go! (LARRABEE *stares at the ground for a long time, and* MAUDE *decides to placate.*) Now, dear, this can be done pleasantly, without hurting anyone. . . .

LARRABEE (*looks up at* DAVID *and speaks quietly and quite pleasantly*): Your mother is concerned for fear I may frighten you by shouting at you. Do you share her concern?

DAVID: No, sir.

LARRABEE: I would be pleased if you would go, Maude. (MAUDE *looks from her son to her husband, makes a moue of resignation, and starts for the house. She stops once, as though to say something, then changes her mind and goes.*) Can you remember back to the last time I shouted at you?

DAVID (*after some thought*): No.

LARRABEE: I will refresh your memory. It was on the *Valiant*. In the Astor Cup Race. I gave an order to jibe, and you were not paying attention.

DAVID: Oh, yes.

LARRABEE: The boom came over and was about to strike you when I shouted. I shouted to save your life.

DAVID (*smiling*): I don't think it will be necessary again.

LARRABEE: Nor do I. Why do you want to marry this girl?

DAVID: Because I'm in love with her.

LARRABEE: How do you know?

DAVID: I know.

LARRABEE: Have you slept with her?

DAVID: No.

LARRABEE: I am glad to see you have the grace to deny it. (*And he goes on, stopping* DAVID's *abortive protest.*) I will say to you what my father said to me when I was younger than you are now. I thought I had said it to you when you were younger, but apparently I was neglectful of my duties. There are two kinds of women in this world: those you sleep with, and those you marry.

DAVID (*angrily*): I haven't slept with her!

LARRABEE: The first denial is sufficient.

DAVID: Look here, father——

LARRABEE (*strongly, cutting him off*): *No* gentleman makes love to a servant in his mother's house!

DAVID: She's not a servant.

LARRABEE: She is a servant's daughter. In behaving as you have, you have not merely betrayed your mother's trust, you have insulted Fairchild, since what you have done is the worst form of condescension. I have too much respect for Fairchild ever to intrude on his personal life; I expect you to have the same respect for his daughter.

DAVID: I have so much respect for his daughter, I want to marry her.

LARRABEE: That's overdoing it. (LINUS *wanders on from the garden.*) And just how did you plan to proceed? Will you have Fairchild drive us to church, then change his clothes and escort the bride down the aisle?

DAVID: That wasn't necessary, father.

LARRABEE (*to* LINUS): I suppose you've heard about this proposed . . . alliance.

LINUS: Yes, I have.

LARRABEE: And I suppose you think it's just dandy.

LINUS: Yes, I do. If it's what David wants. And if it's what Sabrina wants.

LARRABEE (*abruptly*): I am coming in to the office on Monday.

LINUS: What for? Nothing you can do can affect David. His money is his own; his share of the company is his own.

LARRABEE: I understand that nothing I can do, or say, can affect my sons. I am coming in to find out why I am being accused of driving young Matthew Loring to the wall.

LINUS (*his eyes narrowing*): You haven't driven young Matthew Loring to the wall.

LARRABEE: I know I haven't. But my name also happens to be Linus Larrabee and people sometimes fall into error and charge me with the sins of my son.

LINUS (*his eyes alight with the sense of impending battle*): What sins? What have you heard from your fellow mourners? Anyone can tell you've been to church; you're full of the latest Wall Street gossip.

LARRABEE: Don't make cheap jokes. Matt Loring is one of my oldest friends, and one of the most respected men in New York! What do I say to him next time I see him?

LINUS: That his son is a thief.

LARRABEE: That's a lie!

LINUS: Don't say that to me. He tried to take a company of mine—to *TAKE* a company—with a trick that would have made Jay Gould blush with shame. What if Matt Loring's a friend of yours? His son's no friend of mine. He tried to move in on me, and I keelhauled him.

LARRABEE (*shouting*): You needn't have spread our name all over the street!

LINUS: I don't give a damn for the good opinion of the old men you meet at funerals! When I break a man who tried to break me, I want the world to know it!

LARRABEE (*shouting*): Don't sound so damned majestic! Who the hell do you think you are?

And on this, MAUDE *hurries on from the house.*

MAUDE: Linus! You promised not to shout at David!

LARRABEE (*shouting*): I'm not shouting at David, God damn it!

And he falls into a chair, bitter with frustration, but quickly resigned to it.

MAUDE (*to* DAVID): What is it? What's the matter?

DAVID (*disturbed*): A little business conference.

MAUDE (*to* LINUS): I asked you to keep away.

LINUS: I'm sorry. (*To his father.*) If you care to come in on Monday, I'll be glad to go over the entire situation with you, and explain exactly what happened.

LARRABEE (*quietly*): I am no longer interested. (*He looks over at* DAVID.) Are you sure in your own mind? Do you know what you're doing?

DAVID: Yes.

LARRABEE: And you want to do it.

DAVID: Yes, sir.

LARRABEE (*with quiet resignation*): Maude, I will not oppose this marriage. I do not approve of it. I would prevent it if I could. But I will accept it if I have to.

MAUDE: Oh.

A long pause, as LARRABEE *stares off into space, moodily. Then, finally, he glances over at* DAVID.

LARRABEE: This sort of thing wouldn't happen if you'd gone to Harvard.

MARGARET *appears on the terrace.*

MAUDE: Yes, Margaret.

MARGARET: The guest has arrived, madam. Mr. Paul d'Ar—— (*She consults the calling card.*) —d'Ar——

MAUDE: D'Argenson, Margaret. Yes. Will you bring Monsieur——(*She enunciates meticulously, as to a child.*)—— d'Ar-gen-son to us here, please. (MARGARET *goes.* MAUDE *crosses to the foot of the steps as she speaks.*) Now, we'll have no more talk about it. I'll speak to Fairchild the first chance I get. But if this man knows Madge de Lessac, he probably knows other friends of ours. While he is here, I want no mention of Sabrina, and I don't want to hear the word "marriage". I am quite fed up with marriage and consider it a deplorable institution. (*And then, with great charm.*) Ah, Monsieur d'Argenson! (*This, of course, to the guest, who is ushered on to the terrace by* MARGARET, *who then retires.* PAUL d'ARGENSON *is five-foot-eleven, weighs a hundred and sixty pounds, has a lovely moustache, and wears glasses. He is a year or two younger than* LINUS, *and gives the immediate impression of being an affable and good-natured man. He wears a permanent smile that crinkles his eyes behind the heavy, black-rimmed, peculiarly French glasses, and gives that part of his face a slightly Japanese cast. The eyes are alive and perceptive. With his affability, the man has authority. He wears a dark business suit. He crosses the terrace and descends the steps as he speaks, and his accent is rather startling to an American, for it has an overlay of Oxonian English.*)

PAUL: Mrs. Larrabee, how good of you to ask me out. (*They shake hands.*) I do hope you forgive me for calling you on the telephone.

MAUDE: But I was delighted! How dull it would have been to mail the letter and miss the week-end!

PAUL: I am here only a short time, you see, and I have heard so much about you from——oh, the letter!

    He produces it from a pocket.

MAUDE: It was sweet of Madge to send you to me. (*She pockets the letter.*) This is my husband. Linus,—Monsieur d'Argenson.

LARRABEE: How do you do.

    They shake hands.

PAUL: Mr. Larrabee. . . .

MAUDE: My son Linus . . . my son David. . . .

    They shake hands.

LINUS: Hello. . . .

DAVID: Nice to see you.

PAUL: I am most charmed to meet you all. And may I say that it is an imposingly handsome family?

MAUDE: You certainly may; I like to hear it said. I'm sorry our chauffeur couldn't meet you. He was away with Mr. LARRABEE.

PAUL (*with great, happy relief*): Oh, then that was *not* Fairchild!

MAUDE (*puzzled*): No, it was John, the gardener.

PAUL: Oh, yes, the gardener.

LINUS (*examining him carefully*): How did you know our chauffeur's name was Fairchild?

PAUL (*easily*): I believe your mother said on the telephone that I would be met by a man named Fairchild. What a lovely place you have here!

He is looking over at the garage.

MAUDE: Yes, we're very fond of it. That's Long Island Sound, you know.

PAUL: Beautiful!

But his eyes keep returning to the garage.

LINUS: That's the garage.

PAUL (*ignoring that one*): But how lucky you are! It is like having the Riviera an hour from Paris.

MAUDE: Yes, it is. (*And then, in her careful French.*) *Mais, dites-moi, Monsieur, est-ce que vous preferez parler le française?*

PAUL: *Ah, non, madame, vous êtres très aimable,* but I prefer to speak English while I am here. If you can put up with my English.

MAUDE: But it's very good! Did you go to school in England?

PAUL: No, I had an English nanny.

LARRABEE (*abruptly*): Can I get you a drink?

PAUL: Thank you, but I'm afraid it's a bit early in the day for me for spirits.

LARRABEE: Not for me. You'll excuse me.

He starts for the bar.

MAUDE (*gaily*): Oh, but we'll have an apértif before lunch! I think some champagne, Linus! (*To* PAUL.) There's really no apértif like champagne, is there? So much nicer than cocktails.

PAUL: I agree, oh yes!

MAUDE (*calling*): Will you see to it, Linus? And to the wine for lunch? (LARRABEE *grunts and goes into the bar.*) Now, I know you'll want to get rid of some of the soot you acquired on the ride out. Don't you just love our railroad? David, will you take Monsieur d'Argenson up to your room?

MARGARET *comes from the house to get the coffee tray.*

PAUL: Thank you; you are very kind.

The three men start for the house.

DAVID: Did you fly over?

PAUL: Yes. I would have preferred the boat, but there is never enough time these days, is there?

MAUDE: Margaret, would you tell Fairchild I would like to see him?

PAUL'S *head almost snaps around, but he holds it as he sees* LINUS *watching him.* MARGARET *goes off.*

PAUL: What a magnificent view! And all those boats, they are yours?

LINUS: Yes, they are.

PAUL: Ah, yes, I have heard that you are a great family of sailors.

They continue on to the house. LINUS *a step to the rear.*

DAVID: Do you sail?

PAUL: No, skiing and shooting are my sports.

LINUS: Tell me: have you ever shot wild boar in Belgium?

PAUL: Oh, yes! Wonderful sport!

LINUS *nods with satisfaction, and they go into the house.* MAUDE *stands and watches them go, then droops a little and stares out into space, and allows herself, finally, the small, pleasant ache of feeling sorry for herself.* FAIRCHILD *and* MARGARET *appear from the right and approach her, and it is* MARGARET'S *passage to the house that brings* MAUDE *to with a start.*

MAUDE: Oh! Fairchild. Yes. I want to speak to you. (MARGARET *goes into the house.*) Will you sit down? Please. Bring a chair.

FAIRCHILD: No, thank you, madam.

She nods and regards him calmly, with instinctive sureness.

MAUDE: I have something to tell you that is quite personal, and for the time being I'd rather it weren't discussed in the household. I know I can depend on you. It concerns Mister David and Sabrina. (*His eyes show a flash of anxiety, but his face remains expressionless.*) Sabrina hasn't told you.

FAIRCHILD: No, madam.

MAUDE: David came to me this morning and said he wishes to marry Sabrina.

FAIRCHILD: I beg your pardon?

MAUDE: Mr. David wishes to marry Sabrina.

> FAIRCHILD *considers it quietly.* SABRINA *comes dashing on, bubbling over with high spirits. All the doubt and self-searching of the previous evening are gone.*

SABRINA: Linus? (*At sight of them she stops short.*) Oh, I'm sorry. I was looking for Linus.

MAUDE: Sabrina, I've just told your father. (SABRINA *looks blank.*) About you and David.

SABRINA: Oh.

MAUDE: I thought I should consult you, Fairchild, as to how we should proceed.

FAIRCHILD: I'm sorry, madam, I won't have it.

MAUDE (*startled*): What?

FAIRCHILD: Begging your pardon, madam, I'll not hear of it.

MAUDE: Oh! Sabrina, perhaps you'd like to speak to your father alone.

SABRINA (*quickly*): Oh, no!

FAIRCHILD: I mean no offence, madam. I've always liked Mr. David.

MAUDE: Yes, Fairchild, of course. I'm not offended that you oppose the marriage. No. But I'm terribly curious to know *why* you oppose it. And I'm sure Sabrina is, too.

FAIRCHILD (*simply*): I couldn't stand the scandal.

MAUDE: Oh.

FAIRCHILD: Please understand, madam. I've worked hard, these thirty years, at the one job I've wanted, and I've gained the respect of my fellow men. And I'll not see it go. There's no credit for me, or for her, in such a marriage. It's all very well for you and Mr. Larrabee: the papers and all would say how fine and democratic you were to be giving your blessing to the marriage, but nobody would praise Tom Fairchild and call him a democratic man. No. They'd laugh behind my back. And it would be no good

67

trying to tell them that I've got more money than I know
how to use in this life. . . .

MAUDE: Have you, Fairchild?

FAIRCHILD: Yes, madam. But they wouldn't believe it.
And they wouldn't care. Democracy can be a wickedly
unfair thing, madam. Nobody poor was ever called
democratic for marrying somebody rich.

A pause, as MAUDE *considers that one. Then she rouses
herself.*

MAUDE: But Fairchild, if the children defy us . . . surely if
you have that much money . . . after all, you love books
so . . . you could retire, and read.

FAIRCHILD (*shaking his head*): Read in my own time!

The door to the bar opens, and LARRABEE *walks on to the
terrace carrying a drink half gone. They turn as they hear the
door slam.*

MAUDE: Oh. Linus.

LARRABEE: Well?

MAUDE: Fairchild won't hear of it.

LARRABEE: What?

MAUDE: He won't have the marriage. He won't hear of it.

LARRABEE *lets the news sink in. He hefts the glass,
examines it carefully, then addresses it.*

LARRABEE (*quietly*): I can remember, back in the twenties,
when George Bellamy's daughter eloped with the chauffeur.
It was on the front pages of every newspaper in the
country, and the news was cabled abroad. It shook our
world. Now, my son has decided that he wants to marry
our chauffeur's daughter. I am forced to approve. My
wife pretends to be delighted. But the chauffeur . . .
WON'T HEAR OF IT!

*He drains the glass, then with his toe, he pushes a potted
plant off the edge of the terrace. It crashes on the ground
below. He turns calmly and goes back into the bar.* MAUDE
immediately starts after him.

MAUDE: Linus!

FAIRCHILD: Madam, will you explain to him——

MAUDE (*hastily, as she goes*): Yes, Fairchild, of course. It's not democratic.

> *She hurries into the bar.* SABRINA, *who had to clap a hand to her mouth at the conclusion of* LARRABEE'S *speech, has now regained control, and she looks at her father with affection.*

FAIRCHILD (*gruffly*): I *am* sorry. I want you to be happy. But I had to say what was in my mind.

> FAIRCHILD *turns and goes. And now, as* SABRINA *lets the laughter bubble to the surface, she is close to tears at the same time; wild with rage and wild with laughter at the entire situation. She doubles over with horror and laughter, then straightens up and holds her head.*

> DAVID *comes out of the house talking to* LINUS, *who follows a few steps behind.*

DAVID: You certainly were inquisitive. Why all those questions?

LINUS: I just wanted to know something about him.

DAVID: And why did you put in a phone call to Paris?

LINUS: I want to know all about him.

DAVID: Why? (*But then he sees* SABRINA, *and stops short, apprehensive at the way she looks at him.*) Sabrina, I have to talk to you.

SABRINA (*reproachfully*): Oh, David! David! David!

DAVID (*horrified*): Don't tell me you know!

SABRINA: Know! David! You decided you want to marry me, and so you went and asked your mother?

DAVID: Now, wait a minute——

> *He hurries to her.*

SABRINA: And your mother asked your father, and probably asked your brother, and then went and asked her chauffeur! Who just happens to be my father! But there's still the cook and the maid and the upstairs maid and the gardener to ask. When are you going to get around to asking me?

DAVID: Sabrina——

LINUS: David, for God's sake!

> *And he is overcome with laughter.*

DAVID: Now, wait a minute! I don't know how this happened——

SABRINA: But I know. It happened because you took me for granted. Oh, yes. Look deep, David. You took it for granted that I would curtsey and say, "Yes, sir," didn't you?

DAVID: No!

MAUDE *comes out of the bar.*

SABRINA: Of course you did. It never crossed your mind that I might curtsey and say, "No, sir." But it did cross your mind that your mother might say no. And so, of course you spoke to your mother instead of to me.

DAVID: That's not how it happened! I tried to ask you last night, but you kept changing the subject. And then, this morning——

MAUDE: David, do you mean to say you hadn't asked Sabrina? David, how rude!

DAVID (*frantic*): Nobody gave me a chance to ask her! All I did was speak to you out of sheer politeness, because I felt I owed it to you, and the next thing I knew, it was on the agenda of the United Nations!

LINUS (*peremptorily*): Sabrina, what did you find out last night?

SABRINA: What do you care? You took it for granted, too, didn't you?

LINUS (*after a moment, bluntly*): Yes.

SABRINA: And that's what's always been wrong with the story. Everyone takes it for granted that Cinderella will marry Prince Charming when he comes knocking on her door with that diamond-studded slipper. Nobody considers Cinderella. What if she thinks Prince Charming is a great big oaf? Ah, not you, David, you're sweet——

DAVID (*strongly, directly*): Sabrina, I apologise. I love you. You're the only girl in the world for me. I want to marry you. I want you to marry me. Will you?

SABRINA (*trying to smile, she makes a small curtsey*): No, sir.

DAVID (*grimly*): I don't blame you after this.

SABRINA (*tenderly*): Ah, no, not after this. It's not because I'm offended. Thank you for wanting to marry me, David. And thank you again for a beautiful night, and for the chance to find out what I needed to know. I wanted you very much to make love to me last night, did you know that? But you were a gentleman, and by the time you felt you knew me well enough to try, I knew you well enough to know I didn't want you to. Ah, is that cruel?

LINUS (*savagely*): Get rid of those romantic ideas! It doesn't happen that way!

    SABRINA *turns and stares at him.*

SABRINA: What's the matter? Aren't we making the right moves? Shall I take him, not loving him? Is that being realistic in one easy lesson; is that how you make the game come out? Do you know what I think? I don't think you know how to make it come out! I don't think you have another move left!

LINUS (*hard*): You're running away from everything you wanted!

SABRINA: No!

LINUS: All of the world, and love!

SABRINA: No!

LINUS: If you settle for Paris, you're lost!

DAVID (*cutting in, sharply*): Look, if I'm going to be turned down, let me do it on my own, will you?

LINUS: Wait a minute, David. This is important.

DAVID: Why to you?

    And that stops LINUS *dead. Pause.* SABRINA *regards him thoughtfully.*

SABRINA: Yes. Why to you?

    Pause. Then LINUS *looks past* SABRINA *to see* PAUL d'ARGENSON *stroll out on to the terrace.*

LINUS: Miss Fairchild, have you——

    He gestures toward PAUL. SABRINA *turns and looks, stares in disbelief, and shakes her head in horror.*

PAUL: 'Allo, Sabrina, ça va?

SABRINA: Oh, no. Oh, no, no, no, no, no. (*She advances on*

PAUL *murderously*.) How dare you come across the ocean looking for me, and walk in on these people you don't even know? They're having enough trouble with me as it is! Go away! Go home! Go back to Paris!

PAUL: *Mais, ne te faches pas!* I wanted to surprise you!

LINUS: You did.

MAUDE (*quietly*): Sabrina, I think we may assume from this that you and Monsieur d'Argenson are acquainted. But I really don't like having my luncheon guests ordered out of my house.

    And SABRINA, *suffused in mortification, stands there looking helplessly for something to hold on to. Then suddenly she turns, ducks her head, and dashes off toward the garage.*

LINUS (*seeing her heading for that old wooden trellis*): Look out!

    But it is too late. There is a crash, and we hear SABRINA's *voice in a tearful wail.*

SABRINA (*off*): Oh! . . . Ow! . . . Oh!

    LINUS *dashes off toward her, with* PAUL *and* DAVID *right after him.*

THE CURTAIN FALLS

ACT IV

The same, a few seconds later. As the curtain rises, LINUS *is setting* SABRINA *on the wall.*

LINUS: There you are. In the same place. It seems appropriate.

MAUDE: Are you sure she's all right?

LINUS: No bones broken. But quite a scratch on one leg. (*He smiles at* SABRINA.) The same leg . . . I think.

SABRINA: I'd like to go home, please.

> DAVID *hurries on with a pail of water.* PAUL *is right behind him.* LINUS *gets out a clean handkerchief and dips it in the water.*

LINUS: Raise your skirt.

> *No response.*

PAUL: Sabrina, raise your skirt.

> LINUS *waits;* SABRINA *stares at him grimly.*

LINUS (*good-humoured*): Would you rather have David do it? David . . .

> *He hands her leg to* DAVID, *then the handkerchief.* DAVID *holds her leg, then glances at* PAUL, *and hesitates.*

DAVID: Maybe you'd like to——

> *He pushes the leg toward* PAUL.

PAUL: Thank you. (*He makes a move to take the leg, then remembers that he is a guest.*) Oh, no, no. You go ahead.

DAVID (*insistent*): Here.

PAUL: No, it's perfectly all right.

SABRINA: Would you gentlemen kindly stop passing my leg about among you?

> *She pulls her leg away, and takes the handkerchief.*

MAUDE: David, Linus, I think Sabrina and Monsieur d'Argenson would like to talk alone.

> MARGARET *has appeared on the terrace.*

MARGARET: Paris is calling Mr. Linus, madam.

MAUDE: Paris? Linus, there's a long distance call for you from——

LINUS: Yes, mother, I'll take it.

He runs across, and up the steps, and into the house. MARGARET *follows him in, and* MAUDE *starts to follow.*

MAUDE: David——?

DAVID *stares at* PAUL *and* SABRINA *for a moment, then goes into the garden.*

PAUL (*apologetically*): Mrs. Larrabee . . .

MAUDE: No, no.

She goes into the house. PAUL *turns to* SABRINA.

SABRINA: Hello. . . . (*He studies her for a moment, then strides over to her, pulls a small jeweller's box from his pocket, hands it to her, and walks away.*) What is it?

PAUL (*diffidently*): Nothing. A rabbit.

She opens the box and looks.

SABRINA: Ah, Paul! For my bracelet!

She comes off the wall and goes to him.

PAUL (*still slightly injured*): I thought it might please you.

SABRINA: It does! I love it! Thank you, Paul!

He turns and smiles at her.

PAUL: But you do not remember what it is.

SABRINA: Should I? Is it something special?

PAUL: Do you remember your birthday last year? In Dijon. We took a walk in the woods near the house, and when we came home the little gardener's daughter brought you a present. A rabbit.

SABRINA: Oh, yes!

PAUL: And you asked her to take care of it for you, and told her she must call it Peter, because in America all rabbits are called Peter.

SABRINA (*laughing*): How sweet of you to remember. I wonder how Peter is, now.

PAUL: Peter is once again a mother. (*She laughs joyously. He grins.*) Push his tail.

SABRINA: Mmm?

PAUL: Yes! Push his tail!
She does.

SABRINA (*with delight*): He wiggles his ears!

PAUL: But a rabbit must wiggle his ears!

SABRINA: How lovely. (*She touches him gently.*) Thank you, Paul.

PAUL (*a little ruefully*): That was not the welcome I expected.

SABRINA: Oh.

PAUL: One takes a plane because the boat would seem so long, and looks forward so to the meeting, and then—— (*He shrugs.*) Go away. Go home. Go back to Paris.

SABRINA: I'm sorry. I was having trouble with a domestic problem, and I didn't think I'd have to tackle my foreign policy so soon.

PAUL: And what is the domestic problem?

SABRINA: David wants to marry me.
He stares at her for a moment.

PAUL: You have been a busy girl these two weeks. (*But then he retracts.*) No, I can understand his wanting to marry you. But I would not like it if you wanted to marry him.

SABRINA: I don't.

PAUL: It has not gone well, here.

SABRINA: No.

PAUL (*with possessive warmth and gentleness*): Sabrina, when you said you must go back to America, I let you go. I did not want to let you go. But I knew it was something you must do, and I thought: "She will come back soon." But it is already too long. And so I have come across the ocean to tell you that I have missed you.

SABRINA (*affected and pleased*): Did you really come all that distance just to see me?

PAUL: Paris has not been the same without you.

SABRINA (*with deep nostalgia*): Was it lovely the day you left?

PAUL: Yes.

SABRINA: It didn't rain.

PAUL: A little, in the morning.

SABRINA (*far away*): A grey Paris morning . . . and in back of the Madeleine, the old women selling flowers in the rain. . . .

PAUL: Will you come home to Paris, Sabrina?

LINUS *comes out of the house and lopes over to them cheerfully.*

LINUS: How are you getting along with the patient?

PAUL: Oh, fine! Very well. But I'm afraid it was wrong of Sabrina to mislead your brother so.

LINUS: We always blame the woman when a man falls in love, as though no man had the courage of his inclinations.

PAUL: I beg your pardon?

SABRINA'S *eyes open wide with surprise.*

SABRINA: Thank you.

LINUS: You're here on business. I may be able to give you a hand.

PAUL (*a quick wary glance at* SABRINA, *who is tying the handkerchief around her knee, then he smiles at* LINUS.) Why, ah——that is very good of you. I know you, of course. Larrabee Shipping. I wish I had a thousand francs for every bill of lading I have paid to Larrabee Lines.

LINUS: I trust we didn't overcharge you.

PAUL: I am your guest, Monsieur.

LINUS (*with an acknowledging nod*): You're trying to get hold of that new plastic, aren't you? The new process for producing Polyvinyl Chloride.

PAUL: How did you know?

LINUS: It's a great formula: cuts the cost in half.

PAUL (*grudgingly*): Well, I thought while I was here. . . .

LINUS: You're smart to try to tie up the European rights. You'll make a killing.

PAUL (*eagerly*): That I know! But my problem is——(*Then, with a glance at* SABRINA, *who is watching grimly.*) Ah, well, such a thing is not of great importance——

LINUS: It's too bad you found you couldn't do anything about it from Paris. If you had got in touch with me, I'd have saved you the trip.

PAUL: You know the company? (LINUS *nods.*) You are not associated with—— (LINUS *nods.*) You do not own it.

LINUS: I will, on Monday.

PAUL: Oh, *mon Dieu*! And I have been trying for four months! Monsieur Larrabee, I do not expect you to take my word that I am the best man in Europe to handle this. I can give you all the references——

LINUS: I don't need them. I know you're the man. I've inquired.

PAUL: D'*accord*?

LINUS: D'*accord*.

PAUL: Sabrina, did you hear? You have brought me to the one man I came to find. You are my good luck; I have known it always.

SABRINA (*icily*): I'm awfully glad I brought you two together.

LINUS (*easily*): Perhaps I shouldn't have brought up business at this particular time.

PAUL: No, no! Sabrina was making a joke——

SABRINA: Oh!

LINUS: I'll tell you:—my father is chairman of the board and he would want to be consulted on a deal of this sort. He's very much interested in plastics.

PAUL: Yes, I would like to talk to him. He offered me a drink a while ago. . . .

LINUS: You'll find him in the bar having a scoop for himself.

PAUL (*going toward the bar*): Thank you.

LINUS: And then we'll set up a meeting at my office on Monday.

PAUL: You are very kind. (*He smiled over at* SABRINA'S *back.*) Sabrina, you should have told me about him! (*He salutes* LINUS *and goes into the bar.* LINUS *salutes back, then turns to* SABRINA, *who regards him grimly.*)

SABRINA: Why did you do that? (*He comes down to her.*) Do you tamper with everyone's life this way? (*He nods.*) Why?

LINUS: Because I can.

SABRINA: Last night you dangled David in front of me like a . . . carrot, just to see if I would bite. Now you've reversed the process with Paul. You took the carrot away. Why?

LINUS: I'd underestimated you. If you wouldn't settle for David, you don't have to settle for him.

SABRINA: I would like to decide for myself!

LINUS: I should hate to see you domesticated, Sabrina. There are so many wonderful things you want to do.

SABRINA: Do I have to do them alone?

LINUS: If you want to do them at all. Stand still and choose, Sabrina. You're so excited by the things you learned in Paris that you're galloping off in all directions. If you want to see everything and do everything and live an active life in a passive world, you'd better get used to the idea that you have to live it alone.

SABRINA: I suddenly find that I know you better than anyone in this world—but why this terrible compulsion to make me into your own image? If you are the cat that walks alone, must I walk alone, too?

LINUS: It's the only way to be yourself, on your own terms, without the pretensions you picked up in Paris. (*Almost savagely.*) You still can marry your Frenchman. Nothing I've done has changed things. You can still have everything money can buy, and ski all over the map of Europe. If you want to sell out, go sell. Just walk through that door and say yes.

SABRINA: How easy for you to make the challenge. (*Flashing out.*) Will you give everything up? And start with nothing?

LINUS (*grabbing her by the arms*): Any day! The only measure of living is how productive you are. Don't get it confused with money.

SABRINA: Do you honestly think I have?

LINUS: You've discovered that life is an enormous experience that must be used. Will you settle for the very best burgundy?

Pause.

SABRINA (*quietly, after a moment*): No. No. Would you let go of me, please? (*He makes no move. She steps back.*) If

I'm to live on my own terms, that is making a start, isn't it? (*No answer.*) For I must learn to prevent others from imposing their terms on me. And the next step is to impose my terms on others? Isn't that true?

LINUS: Yes.

SABRINA: That takes power.

LINUS: It's the only way to keep alive.

SABRINA: I see. It is the most exciting game in the world, isn't it? With life-size figures. And the one who loves is captured.

LINUS: The answer is: not to love.

SABRINA: And be without love? (*She moves closer.* JULIA *appears from the house and stands on the terrace, watching.*) Have you made your choice, Linus? And is it irrevocable? Power corrupts, you know. And absolute power corrupts absolutely.

LINUS: Where did you get that? Out of a book?

SABRINA (*softly*): I beg you to think that you may be mistaken.

JULIA: Why don't you hit him? It's the only thing he'll understand. (*They turn to her. Her eyes are flashing murderously.*) What are you trying to do to this girl?

LINUS: How do you know I'm trying to do anything?

JULIA: I have a room with a view! You're afraid to take her, and afraid to lose her, so you're warning her off the rest of the world. I don't have to tell you what you're passing up; it's pretty damned clear you know. But you want to own her without being owned. You can't unbend, you won't give in. You're a stiff-necked, self-sufficient, autocratic bastard—— (*She begins to cry.*)——and you've been my favourite man since the day you were born.

LINUS (*taking a step to her*): Aunt Julia——

JULIA (*tearfully*): If you come near me, I'll kick you. What do you want to do. Make her a part of Larrabee Industries? And then fight off your competitors? Just hang a sign around her neck! "Please don't handle the merchandise!" (*She turns to* SABRINA.) And as for you! You listen to me! If anyone tries to tell you that she travels the farthest who

79

travels alone, believe me, when you get there you'll find it wasn't worth the trip! (*She turns on* LINUS.) Get into her life or get out of her life! But don't stand around playing god!

MAUDE *has appeared from the house.*

MAUDE (*concerned*): Julia, what's the matter?

JULIA: The whole trouble is, you didn't beat him enough!
She ducks her head and runs into the house. Pause. MAUDE *stares at* LINUS *coldly.*

MAUDE: Linus, it is almost time for lunch. Have you been sailing, or are you going sailing?

LINUS: I've been sailing, mother.

MAUDE: Then it would please me if you would go and change. I'm quite fond of you in that costume, but I prefer something less rakish for lunch.

LINUS: Yes, mother.
He starts for the house.

MAUDE: And please tell Margaret we'll have cocktails inside in ten minutes.

LINUS: Yes, mother.

MAUDE: Your father ordered up a bottle of champagne. I think we'll need two.

LINUS: Yes, mother.

MAUDE: Where is Monsieur d'Argenson.

LINUS: In the bar, counting his blessings.
He goes in. MAUDE *looks across at* SABRINA.

MAUDE: I want to apologise. I'm only beginning to realise what we have done to you here, these past two weeks.

SABRINA: Ah, no, please. It's nobody's fault but my own. (*And then, almost to herself.*) How silly to think that since I had changed, the world must have changed along with me.

MAUDE: My world is so rigid, and has such a horror of change. I didn't make the rules I live by. I suppose it's cowardly of me to say that, but it's true. They were made for me before I was born.

SABRINA (*with a wry smile*): You forget, I was brought up by those very same rules.

MAUDE: But with none of the fun or advantages. And yet, when you had a chance to move into this world, you said no. (*A moment.*) You knew I didn't want you to marry David.

SABRINA: I guessed.

MAUDE: David is very much like me. The things I want for him are the things he wants for himself: a calm, orderly world; the pursuit of comfort; the avoidance of pain. Is that what you want? (SABRINA *shakes her head.*) Well, then, you're free of our world. Just as Linus is. And if money means that little to you, you're safe. (*She smiles to herself.*) Our world is dying, anyway. Mr. Larrabee claims it is already dead, and that we live on in a cemetery, decorating the graves. I don't like to think that; I won't go to the funerals. But I do think that the world has become . . . unsatisfactory. I trust the next will have more grace and dignity. (*She tosses her head with a small, charming smile of defiance.*) If it doesn't, I shall speak sharply to the proprietor.

SABRINA: I hope it does, for you.

> *They smile at each other fondly, and then the woman takes the girl in her arms and holds her in a long embrace.*

MAUDE: I wish you had been my daughter.

> SABRINA, *moved, crinkles up her eyes with pleasure.*
>
> LARRABEE *comes striding out of the bar.*

LARRABEE: Maude! Maude!

MAUDE (*exasperated*): Oh, Linus, I do wish you'd give up calling me from long distances!

> LINUS *strolls out of the house.*

LARRABEE: Maude, we've got a very strange Frenchman on our hands. He's fallen madly in love with Linus. (*To* LINUS.) What did you do to him?

LINUS: Gave him some money.

LARRABEE (*that's understandable*): Oh. Well. But he's quite an interesting chap. Did you know that they still use horses in France for funerals? In the small towns, that is.

DAVID appears from the garden, holding FAIRCHILD firmly by the elbow, hustling him along. He is alive with delight and excitement. FAIRCHILD is definitely reluctant.

FAIRCHILD: Please, Mr. David, if you don't mind——

DAVID: You can't keep a thing like that a secret! Now don't move. (*He plants FAIRCHILD, and turns on SABRINA with a wide grin.*) Sabrina, your father just came to tell me that he's sorry he turned me down. He's decided he mustn't stand in the way of our happiness.

SABRINA: Oh!

DAVID: But then I told him that you had turned me down, and he thinks it may be because of money. He thinks you might change your mind if you had some money of your own. Is that true?

SABRINA: No.

DAVID: I didn't think so. (*He turns on FAIRCHILD.*) But it still holds. You're not going to back down.

FAIRCHILD (*worried*): No, sir, but——

LARRABEE (*to MAUDE*): Did she turn him down, too? What's wrong with the boy?

DAVID (*grinning*): I'm just not the guy, father. That sort of thing does happen. Even to us. All right, Fairchild.

FAIRCHILD: I'd rather not speak of it now, sir——

DAVID: Don't be so modest! (*He races to SABRINA, takes her by the shoulders, and sits her down.*) Sabrina, you're going to learn something about yourself, and it may come as a shock. But no matter what,—remember, I liked you for yourself.

He runs to the garden. FAIRCHILD turns to him as he goes.

FAIRCHILD: Mr. David——

DAVID: You're on your own, Fairchild!

He runs off. Pause.

LARRABEE: Well, what is it?

And FAIRCHILD, trapped, faces the situation, composes himself as best he can, and addresses the family with simple dignity.

FAIRCHILD: I have told Mr. David that I would like to settle some money on Sabrina.

MAUDE: Ah, that's very sweet, Fairchild, but I'm sure Sabrina wouldn't dream of taking your life's savings.

FAIRCHILD (*quietly*): I would like her to have something of her own, now.

LARRABEE: That's damned decent, Fairchild. What kind of sum did you have in mind?

FAIRCHILD (*simply*): Five hundred thousand dollars.

LARRABEE (*impassively*): Five hundred thousand dollars.

FAIRCHILD: Yes, sir.

LARRABEE: You saved that out of your salary?

FAIRCHILD: Oh, no, sir, I made investments. I'd rather not talk about it——

LARRABEE (*suddenly enraged*): You've run up investments of half a million dollars, and you'd rather not talk about it?
He starts across to FAIRCHILD.

MAUDE: Now, Linus, be calm!

LARRABEE: How the hell could a man in your position——
LINUS *cuts across swiftly, blocks off his father, and regard him calmly.*

LINUS (*quietly*): Do you mind? (*He turns to* FAIRCHILD.) Fairchild, this is all in the family. I'd like to know how you did it.

FAIRCHILD: It wasn't difficult, sir. I came here to drive for your father shortly after I came out of the army, in 1919. And by 1926, Della and I had saved six thousand dollars. And it occurred to me to buy some stocks. At first I bought them outright, but then one day I overheard Mr. Larrabee explain to Mrs. Larrabee why it showed confidence in our country to buy on margin. So, from then on, I did. I was driving you to Newport at the time, I believe, sir.

LINUS: And things went along well.

FAIRCHILD: Yes, sir. Since I invested only in companies I had personal confidence in. Like General Motors. But finally, I began to worry. It didn't seem right to be getting all that money for doing something that any fool could do. And it seemed rather a revolting spectacle to see money making money, like small animals breeding in dark corners. I beg your pardon, madam. (*To* LINUS.) And so I sold out.

LINUS: When did you sell out?

FAIRCHILD: Early in October, 1929.

> LINUS *has to work hard to keep from laughing.* LARRABEE *looks murderous.*

MAUDE: But Fairchild! You could have retired! You didn't have to work here!

FAIRCHILD (*mopping his brow*): But I *wanted* to work here!

LINUS (*back to him*): And so you sold out, put your money in the bank, and never went near the market again.

FAIRCHILD: No, sir, I went back in. This is very difficult, Mr. Linus.

LINUS: Well, here, sit down.

> *He moves in a chair.*

FAIRCHILD: Thank you, sir.

> *He sits.*

LINUS: So you went back into the market.

FAIRCHILD: Yes, sir. In 1932. I was sorry to see the stocks of such fine companies fallen so low. I felt I should help by buying as much as I could.

LARRABEE (*howling*): Oh, that was *good* of you!

FAIRCHILD: But this time, I didn't buy on margin. I bought the stocks and put them away.

LINUS: What about that revolting spectacle of money making money, like small animals breeding in dark corners?

FAIRCHILD: I overcome my revulsion, sir. Then, too, I wanted to show my loyalty to the family in its time of trouble.

LARRABEE (*alert*): What do you mean?

FAIRCHILD: The family firm was in quite some difficulties at the time, sir. As you may remember. Mr. Linus was still in college, and had not yet come into the firm.

LARRABEE: Don't rub it in.

LINUS (*cutting in*): And so to show your loyalty to the family, you——

FAIRCHILD: Yes, sir. I bought some Larrabee Shipping.

LINUS: How much?

FAIRCHILD: Seven thousand shares.

LINUS: Seven thou——! (*And now he drives on with intensity.*) Fairchild. Those seven thousand shares. You kept them. You put them away.

FAIRCHILD: Yes, sir.

LINUS: And after I came into the company, and we began to expand into other things:—every time I split that stock, every time I recapitalised, you went along.

FAIRCHILD: I had great confidence in you, Mr. Linus.

LINUS: And you still own it all.

FAIRCHILD: Yes, sir.

LINUS (*driving on*): Fairchild, you don't have to answer this. Would it be presumptuous of me to suggest that you are worth around a million dollars?

FAIRCHILD: That is true, sir.

LINUS: Am I pushing you too hard if I suggest that it is over a million?

FAIRCHILD: When I last looked, it was *just* over a million, sir.

LARRABEE: Fairchild, you're fired!

FAIRCHILD (*injured*): I hope you don't mean that sir. *I* didn't want to speak of it.

MAUDE: Oh, no, Fairchild, I'm really provoked at you. Think of your family! Think of what you could have done for Della and Sabrina!

FAIRCHILD: If Della had lived, madam, I know I'd have done something about it. But most of this happened after she died. And I was happy here. But you may be right about Sabrina.

He looks at his daughter.

SABRINA (*happily, quite overcome with love and laughter*): I wouldn't have wanted it any other way. (*And then she can't help it: she runs to him and holds him tight.*) Bless you.

FAIRCHILD *disengages, rather embarrassed.*

FAIRCHILD (*to* MAUDE): You'll excuse me, madam. (*To* SABRINA.) Whatever you choose to do, the money's yours.

SABRINA: Thank you, father. It'll come in handy.

FAIRCHILD *goes. Dead silence. Then* LARRABEE *turns, suddenly, and crosses swiftly to the bar.*

MAUDE: Linus!

LARRABEE: For thirty years he sat in the front seat, and never gave me a tip.

He goes into the bar.

SABRINA (*with a wide, rueful, despairing smile*): What do you know! I'm an heiress!

MAUDE: How wonderful for you, Sabrina! But you must be careful, now, not to let anyone marry you for your money!

SABRINA (*laughing*): I won't. Besides, I'm beginning to think the world is divided into two kinds of men: those you can marry and don't want to; those you want to marry and can't.

MAUDE (*suspecting*): Is there someone you want to marry?

SABRINA: Yes.

MAUDE: Who is it?

SABRINA (*turning to* LINUS): Him.

LINUS: For God's sake, Sabrina, watch your grammar.

SABRINA: It is he.

MAUDE (MARGARET *appears on the terrace*): Yes, Margaret, thank you. (MARGARET *goes.*) Sabrina, if I were your mother I would oppose this vigorously. But since I am Linus' mother, I'm going in to drink a glass of champagne. (*Before she enters the house, she pauses to look back at them.*) It should be interesting, Linus. You want to conquer the world; she wants to love it to death. (*She considers for a moment.*) Either way, it'll be an improvement. (*She goes in.*)

Pause. SABRINA *moves down to the hassock, and sits.*

LINUS (*after a long moment, softly*): How's your knee?

*No answer. He crosses to her, takes the bloodstained hand-
kerchief from her, puts it in his pocket, takes out a clean
handkerchief, and kneels before her. He waits; she raises her
skirt. He swabs the wound, then forms the handkerchief into
a bandage, and ties it about her knee, and his hands rest there
for a long moment. He looks up. Somehow, although it does
not seem as though she has moved, their heads are closer together than before, and it seems impossible not to kiss. They
do, gently and briefly, then part. He doesn't move a muscle,
but one senses that if he were to let go, he would quiver like a
stuck pig. A moment, then he lowers the skirt over her knee,
rises and moves away.*

SABRINA: Haven't you the courage of your inclinations,
Linus? (*No answer.*) Won't you incline my way?

LINUS (*with a glint of a smile*): Sabrina, you keep forgetting
one thing: you don't have to marry anyone.

SABRINA: Oh, yes! I'm not the kind to be alone. I should
always have a husband or a small animal about.

LINUS: I'm sure mother would give you back your singing
cockatoo.

SABRINA: But his talents are so limited! Will you marry me,
Linus? No! Wait! Don't answer that! I'm ahead of
myself!

LINUS (*grinning*): I think so, too.

SABRINA (*taking a deep breath*): Linus. Do you love me?

LINUS (*almost angrily*): You're so peremptory, Sabrina!

SABRINA: Do you!

LINUS (*peremptorily*): Yes!
    She sighs with relief.

SABRINA: Ah, that's good! (*But then she looks anxious*): But
you don't believe in marriage.

LINUS: Yes, I do. It's why I've never married.
    She looks over at him with deep, happy love.

SABRINA: That's terribly romantic!

LINUS: Is it? (*He's rather startled.*) Yes, it is. But Sabrina, I
was never so romantic, or so ambitious, as to aspire to the
richest chauffeur's daughter in the world.

87

SABRINA: You mustn't make fun of my new position in life. It would be the climax to your career. Linus. . . .

She looks at him with a pleading smile. He smiles back gently.

LINUS: If mother is right: if I want to take the world with power, and you want to take it with love, which of us will conquer the world, you or I?

SABRINA (*moving to him*): Neither of us . . . alone.

LINUS: And that's why I should marry you.

SABRINA: That, and because when you put your hand on my knee, you shook . . . a little.

He takes her and lifts her on to the wall.

LINUS: "Sabrina Fair, listen where thou art sitting. Under the glassy, cool, translucent wave" . . . do I have it right?

SABRINA: Yes.

LINUS: Sabrina, will you save me from a fate worse than death?

SABRINA: What?

LINUS: To be domesticated.

SABRINA: Ah, I thought you might say: to be without love.

LINUS: And that, too. Will you save me, Sabrina? You are the only one who can.

SABRINA: "Gentle swain . . . at thy request . . . I am here."

He leans forward and takes her in his arms.

THE CURTAIN FALLS

Further titles in preparation.   All prices subject to alteration.